MARTIN YESTERDAY

MARTIN YESTERDAY

Brad Fraser

NeWest Press
Edmonton

Canadian Cataloguing in Publication Data

Fraser, Brad, 1959–
  Martin yesterday

A play.
  ISBN 1-896300-26-X

  I. Title.
PS8561.R294M37 1998   C812'.54   C98-910684-5
PR9199.3.F7175M37 1998

Cover and interior design: Brenda Burgess

NeWest Press gratefully acknowledges the support of the Department of Canadian Heritage, and the Canada Council for the Arts for our publishing program.

The Canada Council | Le Conseil des Arts
FOR THE ARTS | DU CANADA
SINCE 1957 | DEPUIS 1957

Photographs have been reproduced with the kind permission of the following: David Hawe, Ian Jackson, and Robert Shannon. Author photo courtesy of David Hawe.

Every effort has been made to trace the ownership of copyright material used in this book. The publisher welcomes any information regarding references or credit for attribution in subsequent editions.

Printed and bound in Canada

NeWest Publishers Limited
Suite 201, 8540-109 Street
Edmonton, Alberta T6G 1E6

For Daniel MacIvor

Contents

SAYING THE THINGS PEOPLE DON'T WANT TO HEAR

All of my plays have come from very personal places. This was definitely the case with *Martin Yesterday*. I never wanted to write this play. But in the end, as is the case with all plays that actually get finished, *Martin Yesterday* demanded to be written.

I had been romantically involved with an older, well-established man who represented himself as one thing and turned out to be something completely different. The relationship was difficult and, in the end, imploded after this gentlemen was accused of doing something rather nasty to a young man I was led to believe he had a completely different relationship with. The entire, short-lived affair was further complicated by the fact that the gentleman was infected with HIV. This dangerous complication brought a lot of very complex and confusing issues and questions that for me had been only theoretical into sudden and sometimes frightening actuality.

I tried very hard to let go of this incident in my life and move on to newer and better things, but there were too many unanswered questions, too many missed details that kept the picture incomplete. My mind, being the mind of a writer, began to fill in the gaps with logical possibilities of the imagination. Still, I fought this one hard. It was all too sordid. I couldn't write about a sexual assault between males. I couldn't write about responsibility and culpability as related to HIV infection. I couldn't write a play that was as strange and slippery as what I had just been party to. But it wouldn't go away.

It was around this time that more and more people began to tell me stories that were alarmingly similar to my own. Stories about people knowingly infecting others with the HIV virus. Stories about guys who were having unprotected sex everywhere they could. Stories of other sexual assault accusations. Stories about heartbreaking lies. Stories about willful deception.

Then I went to the Black and Blue Party in Montreal.

The Black and Blue is a huge gay party. It's very much about music and drugs and sex. The boys are buff. The music is pounding. The sweat is free-flowing. The experience is intense.

I met a young guy at this party and took him back to my hotel room. At some point, while we were tangled together in the bed he whispered to me that he wanted me to fuck him bareback.

I don't know what disturbed me more. The fact that he wanted to have sex minus a rubber or the fact that I was so turned on by the idea. Years of seeing friends become infected and sick with AIDS have forced me to change my sexual habits and adopt the condom for anything anal. But the boy's suggestion was so shockingly novel, so horrifyingly nostalgic, that I had to consider it.

It was tempting. Something inside of me whispered, "If it hasn't happened by now it's probably never going to. Just this once. Remember what it was like. He's probably not infected. Do it." It would have been so easy to listen to that voice and follow its erotic urging. But I knew I would wake up the next day riddled with guilt and worry. I'd race to my doctor for an HIV test and spend three weeks thinking about nothing but the test results and how I'd have to make up some story about contracting the virus through oral sex. I demurred the invitation to unprotected sex.

When I asked him why he wasn't worried about passing on or being infected with HIV, he shrugged absently and said, "They say it takes ten years before you even know you've got it and that's a long time. Then you have another ten years of being sick before you die and I'll be like forty-five then so who cares? Anyway people are living longer with it now. Maybe they'll even have a cure." He finished, "I figure we're all gonna be HIV positive anyway." He'd summed up a huge portion of the attitude I'd seen in the gay community since semi-relocating to Toronto a few years ago and had captured all of the issues that had been on my mind since the unfortunate relationship: fear, self-hatred, HIV burnout, optimism, fatalism and the need for a certain kind of physical contact that can suppress all common sense. I was left with one thought: "Write the play."

About this time, on a trip to London, I met with Hilary Norrish, the head of BBC radio drama. We discussed the possibility of my writing a radio play for the Beeb and I tossed the rough story idea for *Martin Yesterday* at her. We decided that I would do a ninety-minute version for radio.

Another motivation for the play was a referendum held in the predominantly French province of Quebec. For the first time I was forced to face the possibility that my country, as I have known it for my entire life, could change quite drastically. This realization spurred further questions about partnership, minority status and individuality, all of which fed my thoughts on the script.

From its inception I rather strongly suspected that very little about the writing of this play would be easy. I knew the straight press was going to have a problem with it. I'd seen the first hints of this during the success of *Poor Super Man*. The entire subtext of that play was the creation of a theatrical world where straight men and women were made to feel like the minority for a change. I wanted the straight audience, as they watched the play, to feel uncomfortable with the way they were being represented. I wanted them to feel the way gay people do when they watch yet another gay or lesbian stereotype mince or lumber across a television, stage or movie screen. I wanted them to face the same indifference to their stories and feelings that gay people face every day.

Reaction to *Poor Super Man*, as with *Unidentified Human Remains and the True Nature of Love* before it, was sharply divided. There was no middle ground. This hidden dynamic coupled with issues that some members of the press seemed to find "overly homosexual" gave a friction to the public reaction to the play that I found both offensive and invigorating.

This queasy, hardly recognized homophobia was summed up perfectly in an interview about *Poor Super Man* that I did for radio. The interviewer, referring to some of the negative press the show had received in Montreal, asked me when I was going to write a play for straight people. I explained, rather sharply, that I generally wrote as many straight, bi or whatever characters as I did gay ones, but being a gay man, it made sense I would do it from a gay perspective. The interviewer hastened to assure me he couldn't have been patronizing me. He was gay too. I found that fact neither reassuring nor surprising. Still, I knew what those people who weren't connecting with the play were really saying even if they weren't saying it. They were saying they felt left out. It wasn't about them. And if it's not about them then they just can't get into it.

Luckily the essential humanity of all the characters in *Poor Super Man* coupled with the heartbreak and outright sentimentality of a noble transsexual character's death of AIDS-related causes, counteracted most of these criticisms. As well, *Poor Super Man* contains only one truly gay character and four other characters of varying sexuality. It was about the gay world meeting the straight world and included enough of the straight world to keep the hets interested. They are, after all, the majority.

I realized early on that this was not to be the case with *Martin Yesterday*. No matter how much I "opened it up" and tried to contextualize what was happening with the world of the play against events in the everyday world, its main concerns would be seen as specifically homosexual. HIV transmission. Sexual assault between males. Perverted father images. Reinventing the family. There wasn't a lot here straight people would want to admit to relating to, even if they did relate. Realizing that, I decided to set the action in the Church/Wellesly gay ghetto of Toronto and the characters would all be men. I hoped making the show ultra-specific would make it ultra-universal.

I was also aware that *Martin Yesterday* was going to tread into some of the same thematic areas as *Poor Super Man*. That earlier play is about all of the positive and noble things that came out of people directly affected by the AIDS crisis. I wrote it for all the truly heroic people I knew, infected or not, who are a part of this epidemic. *Poor Super Man* is often incorrectly identified as a play about people dying of AIDS. Nothing could be further from the truth. *Poor Super Man* is a play about people living with AIDS. There's an important difference.

Martin Yesterday is the other side of that story: a recounting of how difficult it can be to live in a world riddled by disease, death and sexual paranoia. I decided to continue Matt's story, picking it up at a later date, after he'd come out and was integrating himself into Toronto's gay community. To my mind, *Martin Yesterday* is a bookend to *Poor Super Man*, the opposite side of a coin, the darker and negative face of the same issues.

Not including a female in the earlier versions was rather like trying to write a symphony with only half the instruments. I was also at risk of excluding a major portion of my audience. However I felt an important point that I wanted to make with the play was how fucked-up things can get when someone lives in a world that rejects either half of the population. Living in the gay ghetto in Toronto where the male and female contingents of the community barely mix at all had made me sensitive to this.

The video component I was planning to incorporate into the stage version was another challenge. Video is a notoriously cold medium and there is always a danger it will not stylistically mix with the hottest medium of all, live theatre. I hoped the video images would allow me to dispense with traditional theatrical exposition and inform both the characters and the situations within the play on that almost subliminal level video is able to achieve in the lexicon and landscape of our society.

I also knew the script was going to offend a certain segment of the gay community. It's with good reason that many within the community scrutinize the media for unfair and stereotypical depictions of homosexual characters. To question unfair and misleading representations of any group of people is good. But there is a danger, all too frequently faced these days, of being so sensitive to the needs of a particular group or community that instead of well-rounded, interesting characters we are represented by characters who are as compelling as dishwater.

Some people, members of whatever specific community, will never be happy with any character who belongs to their community unless that character is a combination saint and superman. One doesn't write anything with any measure of honesty without hearing from this segment. They will never be placated by anything but absolute homogeneity. I believe that homogeneity devalues any community and I will have no part of it. I write about people as I see them. Not as I wish they were.

So those were the challenges. Straight men won't like it because they're not represented. Women won't like it because they're not represented. Half of the gay audience won't like it because they won't like the way they're represented. The media is almost guaranteed to hate simply because I wasn't structuring it like conventional theatre. I've always loved a challenge.

I fired off the first draft radio script to Hilary. Her reaction was enthusiastic but slightly guarded. She asked a number of difficult questions and, in posing these questions, helped me to define the show and my intentions with it.

Response to a revised script was favourable, enthusiastic even. CBC radio committed to co-producing the radio show.

I did another rewrite of a stage version and had my agent send it out to the usual interested theatrical parties. This procured a one-day workshop from Canadian Stage thanks to their wonderful dramaturge, Iris Turcott. The workshop was very helpful. I'm a great believer in the workshop as a tool in developing a new play. However no other theatres that received the play seemed particularly keen to workshop the show further. Many didn't even respond to the script.

In Toronto I live on the same block as Buddies in Bad Times Theatre, the continent's largest gay theatre. It's not a place I had been invited to work, despite having offered a number of projects to them. On certain levels, I was relieved by this. Despite the fact that I am a gay writer, the idea of being produced at a specifically gay theatre had only moderate appeal for me. Frankly, while I have no problem being an out gay man, I have conflicted desires at being labeled a gay writer who writes for gay theatres. One of my main frustrations with the theatre as opposed to more populist art forms is the sense that one is already preaching to the converted. It seems to me that creating gay theatre for an almost exclusively gay audience only exacerbates this problem.

One day I bumped in Sarah Stanley, the new artistic director at Buddies. We introduced ourselves and chatted. I gave her a brief synopsis of *Martin Yesterday*. She liked the pitch and asked me to drop a copy by her office. I'd liked Sarah immediately and I figured, given the rather specific world the play lived in, Buddies might be a good place to have it produced despite my reservations about a gay theatre. This was after all, the gayest play I'd written.

Sarah offered me the opportunity to direct the show in the opening slot of the next season. I thought it over. My main concern was with the mainstream audience. My history in the theatre has been very much about making my presence known in theatres that, while open-minded and tolerant, are not particularly well-known for producing gay-themed works. How that audience might feel actually driving to the gay ghetto and seeing one of my works in a "gay" theatre weighed on my mind. Ultimately I decided that a production at Buddies would be worth the risk. If *Martin Yesterday* couldn't play at Buddies it probably couldn't play anywhere.

The knowledge that the show would premiere at Buddies in Bad Times began to colour my directorial ideas for the production. If I was going to produce the show in a gay neighbourhood then I wanted the production to reflect that world as much as I could. I wanted to make the show as disorienting, erotic, crazy, brutal and sensation-loaded as the world it would be performed in. I wanted the Buddies production to be unique in both script and production. A one-off show for a very specific audience.

In writing the radio script I had played around with the timeline of the play, setting certain scenes in the present and others in the past, sometimes simultaneously. I wanted to take this effect even further for the stage show. I wanted the play and the production to reflect the chaotic, fractured pattern of everyday life. I wanted to inundate the audience with information and emotion and impart to them some of the roller coaster madness that is the everyday life for some gay people, and I suppose straight as well. I didn't want the show to be reasoned and intellectual. I wanted it to be angry and confrontational. I didn't want to soften anything in order to make it palatable to a more conservative audience. I wanted to use the video component aggressively. I didn't want to pretend to answer profound questions with trite, easy answers. I didn't want to tie everything up in a nice, neat package. I didn't want to resolve all of the plot threads. I didn't want to have each of the characters somehow redeemed at the end of the show. In short, I didn't want to do any of the things one is supposed to do in the creation of a "good" play. I figured if I was going to do a show that would alienate nearly everyone, I might as well go all the way. Besides I'd already proven, a number of times, that I could make a well-made play. It was time for something different.

In rehearsal, as always with a new play, some problems appeared. The characters seemed slightly thin and somehow distant against the immensity of the set and the large video screen that dominated stage left. I wasn't sure that we were getting to know the characters well enough to support the distance they had to go as people. The actors playing Matt and Martin did not seem to be connecting in a genuine way. I was unsure at this point whether this was a problem of the script, the direction, the actors or (as it would ultimately prove to be) a combination of the three. Despite these misgivings I still felt the play and the production packed a wallop and were quite unlike anything usually seen in the theatre. I had made it clear from the beginning of the process that, this being the first production of a new play, I fully intended to continue working on the script after the show had opened. This is when I intended to address some of the problems we'd found but not been able to deal with in rehearsal.

It was too late to do anything else. I'd made commitments to a particular kind of multi-media production that was meant to reflect the carnal, carnival atmosphere that was sometimes life in the contemporary world as seen from the gay perspective. I knew the characters were underdeveloped, immature and not particularly likable, but there was a reality to this fact that I thought fit the play very well. After all, it was set in Toronto. Longish segments of the show were performed in the nude as the characters related to one another in a way that was true to the way lovers relate in life. The sex was evocatively lit and very convincing. Our ejaculating penile prop, with careful body placement and convincing reactions, was a hit with some and a bomb with others. The movement between scenes, the actual roller coaster effect which usually stopped the show, all came together to create the production I had envisioned.

The press reaction ranged from bewildered to hateful. Pretty much what I'd expected.

I told a story to a particular audience in its own vocabulary and, in doing so, excluded and alienated all of those people I had expected to alienate, most of whom were writing for major newspapers. It never seemed to occur to these theatre reviewers that my intention might have been to alienate them. They saw their inability to connect with the material as my failure. I saw it as theirs.

All of this was probably best illustrated by the overblown reaction to a single bit of video in the show. Martin's monologue at the end of the first act about killing his friend with AIDS was delivered in front of images of the prisoners and bodies in the Nazi concentration camps projected onto the screen. Every straight reviewer made a point of singling this moment out as exploitive and tasteless. The *Globe and*

Mail was particularly upset by this imagery. The reviewer capped off her toxic bouquet of sniffy, middle-class comments by citing this Holocaust imagery as the worst thing in a very bad play and an excellent reason for not attending the show. How could I dare to compare the contemporary gay experience with the Holocaust? Apparently, like many of the allegedly well-educated, open-minded people who write for and read our major papers, she was unaware that thousands of gay people died in the camps along with so many others. Those who survived the Nazi purge were not freed after the Allied liberation. They were put back in prisons and hospitals because they were gay. Apparently these journalists are also unaware that the AIDS epidemic has wrought a multitude of related conditions not unlike the survivors' syndrome of those who lived through the Holocaust.

Not all of their criticism was off the mark though. After a break to let the actors claim the show, we started rehearsing again.

I felt that the video conceit made it easy for the audience to disengage from the action of the play. In a play that was already quite challenging, staged in a production that was intentionally frenetic and fragmented, the video was one dazzling production element too many. I pared back to only what was absolutely necessary to retain the integrity of the design and production.

I also felt that the relationship between Matt and Martin wasn't developed or detailed enough. I think perhaps, at that time, I was still too close to the actual source relationship and was having trouble allowing my characters to live their own stories. I made a number of cuts and wrote an entirely new end for the first act.

Because of the restaging needed to realize these alterations to the production, the Nazi concentration camp footage was cut from the show. This was not cut because it offended people. I'd learned a lot from that issue and had plans for it in the next draft of the show.

Nor did I cut the very graphic ass fucking/cum shot scene that opened the show because it offended people. In fact, it seemed to turn on as many people as it offended. From the beginning I knew this sequence might be a problem. However, even though it was very sexy and I was proud as hell of it, I axed it because we were blowing our wad too soon and prolonging the beginning of the show. It left us nowhere to go.

Having gotten the first production out of my system, having

indulged my directorial impulses to the max, I now ripped *Martin Yesterday* apart and began to rewrite and rebuild it.

In the radio version of the play as well as the Buddies production, all of the characters had names beginning with M: Matt, Martin, Michel, Max, and Manny. This ultimately proved to be confusing. Everyone but Matt and Martin got new names.

I cut Manny, Matt's best friend, business partner and the nominal straight character, from the script entirely and replaced him with a character named Rachel. I added this female character to the play for a number of reasons. Most of the women I spoke to who had seen the play seemed to appreciate the show but were unable to really connect to it. The world of *Martin Yesterday* was too exclusive to truly draw them into the concerns of the characters. There was a quiet, sullen thread of resentment I sensed in much of the female reaction, particularly in the press, that I believe had to do with the feeling that a number of "female issues" were being appropriated into a gay milieu. Those people who like to believe that victimization only happens to specific groups of minorities and see certain issues as belonging to some and not others were not impressed with the play. I had no desire to compromise for these people, but I did want women to feel that their concerns were being represented.

Rachel was invaluable with this. She also helped to open up the male characters in a way Manny hadn't. Men, even gay men, talk, act and generally behave differently around women. Some of them actually become more relaxed and vulnerable. I missed this interaction in early drafts of the play and being able to work with a female character changed the entire show for me. The discovery and development of Rachel as a character helped to define and hone the play's themes. In a story concerned with minorities and their possible responsibility for their own status, it made much more sense for one of the characters to be a woman rather than a straight man. Introducing Rachel into the story was suddenly like finding a whole new range of emotions and concerns that enriched the story and the world of the play.

Elements of the earlier version got new lives. The only video left in the show was the roller coaster scene, which would now have an act two counterpart. Matt and Rachel have a fight that encapsulated the press's reaction to the Holocaust footage. Rachel became a much more active and ambitious part of the comic book team than Manny had been. I allowed Matt and Martin to matter to one another more, to have more at stake, moving the story even farther away from its origins. The graphic sexuality was pared back to ensure people could not pretend to be offended by nudity when they were actually offended by other things. The AIDS concerns, which had changed radically with the introduction of protease inhibitors, were updated. This too changed the play's ideas, making it less about a fatal disease and more about responsibility.

It was like writing a brand new play that told the same story from a different point of view. It was an amazing experience. The radio show was radically different from the Buddies show and now the Edmonton production would be radically different from the Toronto production. Each version had a style and perspective that was unique. I found the entire experience a bit like a recurring dream featuring a slightly different cast of characters and radically different landscapes.

The Edmonton production at Theatre Network was a pleasure to rehearse. It wasn't easy but it was professional, challenging and intense. The cast was committed, trusting of the play and my process and I thought we turned in an impressive production of great clarity. As with Toronto, we all brought our best assets to the table and contributed them to the play. The show wasn't a popular success, but considering the general apathy that's infected my home town these last few years, I wasn't surprised.

I came away from the experience with mixed feelings. I was elated and satisfied with what we had all accomplished in a short period of time. I was depressed by the fact that so much of the way we create and market theatre hasn't changed since my introduction to the theatre in the Seventies. And I was both saddened and hardened by the knowledge that I still had to do one last rewrite of *Martin Yesterday* before I let it go.

This final draft was for Martin. I had made a concerted effort to make sure that this character was treated fairly, that he never be a villain or less sympathetic than the other characters. Perhaps because the seeds of his identity were found in someone who had hurt me, I wasn't as successful at doing this with Martin as I was with the other characters. I knew he still wasn't quite there. It was crucial we see why Matt might fall in love with this guy, but I still hadn't allowed Martin to be lovable enough. So I returned to Toronto from Edmonton and rewrote the show one last time. And I hope I finally let the title character have his play.

Despite its turbulent history, *Martin Yesterday* has brought me many gifts. Unlike *Remains* and *Poor Super Man* they have not, so far, been gifts of riches and acclaim. This play's gifts have been more subtle but no less valuable. In the creation and production of this play I have learned more about the theatre, the media, the gay community and myself than with any of the other plays. I feel like I know the world in a way I hadn't known it before. Being a playwright, I don't see how that can be anything but beneficial to all future endeavours.

I hope time and distance will judge this play less harshly than the Canadian reviewers have. Most of these reviews have been laced with a pervasive sense of disappointment. Disappointment that the majority of people who saw the show didn't see themselves represented in it. Disappointment that I still have not produced that great socially acceptable play that the critics will love and that will fill every mid-sized regional theatre on the face of the earth. Disappointment that I don't write the things they want me to write in the way that they wish I would write them. I feel no regret at their disappointment. Those who judge me on their terms instead of my own will almost always be disappointed.

I think *Martin Yesterday* will eventually find its place. It's not a pleasant play. It's not an optimistic play. It's not a play that says something ultimately positive about much of humanity or our society. It depicts a highly suspect morality. It makes some emotionally demanding statements. It provokes debate, much of it bitter. It incenses some and vindicates others. It makes some people laugh. It makes some people cry. And it makes some people very, very angry. In fact, it does everything I believe good theatre is supposed to do.

I think the fact that so many arts reporters seem to view this as a bad thing says far more about the current state of the theatre, theatrical criticism and our society than it does about my limitations as a playwright. I also hope the straight world someday realizes that whatever is happening in the gay world is a precursor to what awaits them. Our societies are really identical but the gay one is more concentrated and intense. I think that someday people will judge *Martin*

Yesterday on its merits as a drama, rather than on their disapproval of the characters and their lifestyles. This will happen when the pervasive homophobia that runs throughout our society is finally addressed and conquered. When that happens perhaps I finally will write that broadly appealing play the straight press keeps hoping for. Or maybe I already have. They just haven't recognized it yet.

Brad Fraser
Toronto, June 1998

DAVID HAWE

Steve Cumyn as Matt, Jean Philippe Côté as Michel, and Rod Wilson as Manny. Buddies in Bad Times Theatre, Toronto.

Martin Yesterday was originally commissioned by the BBC as a radio play, and was co-produced by BBC and CBC Toronto, and directed by Hilary Norrish, in 1997.

Martin Yesterday first premiered as a stage play at Buddies in Bad Times Theatre in Toronto, Ontario in October 1997, with the following cast:

Matt   *Steve Cumyn*
Martin   *Stewart Arnott*
Michel   *Jean Philippe Côté*
Max   *Trevor McCarthy*
Manny   *Rod Wilson*

Assistant Director   *Charles Pavia*
Production Manager   *Sean Baker*
Set/Lighting Design   *Stephan Droege*
Costume Design   *Vikki Anderson*
Composer   *Paul Jacobs*
Sound Designer   *Evan Turner with Sam Shaw*
Video Designer   *David Brindle, Treehouse Productions Inc.*
Video Consultant   *Laurie-Shawn Borzovoy*
Multi-Media Operator   *Adrienne 'Sparky' Whan*
Props Co-ordinator   *Nina Okens*
Stage Manager   *Nan Shepherd*

A highly revised version of *Martin Yesterday* premiered at Theatre Network in Edmonton, Alberta in May 1998, with the following cast:

Matt   *Peter Wilds*
Martin   *Robert Ouellette*
Rachel   *Stephanie Wolfe*
Yves   *Bradley Moss*
Rex   *Chris Fassbender*

Production Manager   *Bruce Hennel*
Set/Lighting Design   *David Skelton*
Costume Design   *Robert Shannon*
Composer   *Paul Jacobs*
Technical Director/Audio Engineer   *Colin Page*
Video Designer   *David Brindle*
Stage Manager   *Ingrid Kottke*

Both productions were directed by Brad Fraser.

MARTIN YESTERDAY

The Characters:

Matt, a man, 33
Rachel, a woman, 33
Martin, a man, 45
Yves (pronounced eve), a man, 30
Rex, a man, 23

The Setting

Toronto, various locations but primarily Matt and Rachel's studio and Martin's condo. Scenes and transitions, as indicated in the script, overlap and dovetail throughout the play.

Production Notes

Please observe pauses only where they have been indicated in the script.

Special thanks to Toronto Councilman Kyle Rae, director Edward Roy, and Iris Turcott at Canadian Stage for advice and support.

French translation provided by Maryse Warda of Théâtre de Quat'Sous in Montreal.

SpumBoy, Fridge Magnet Girl, and all related characters © copyright 1996 Brad Fraser.

Act One

The studio. Matt and Rachel are working. Matt turns to Rachel,
pulling a page from his drawing board and handing it to her.

Matt: The last five pages. Pencils complete.

Rachel: Just in time.

Rachel pulls a fully inked page from her drawing board and hands it
to Matt to examine.

Matt: Hank called. We sold six hundred thousand issues last
month.

Rachel: Six hundred thousand. Excellent. This looks great.

Matt: He also wants to talk to us about a second, bi-monthly
book.

Rachel: C'mon Matt. We can't handle a second book.

Matt: We could if we put another creative team together.

Rachel: Someone else writing and drawing the adventures of
SpumBoy and Fridge Magnet Girl? I don't fucking think so.

Matt: You got a joint rolled?

Rachel: We're out. I just called Billy for delivery.

Matt: I'm jonesing hon.

Rachel: Rough night?

Matt: Went to the Bijou.

Rachel: What's that?

Matt: This sex bar on Gerrard.

Rachel: I wish straight people had sex bars. Nice ones. With candle-
light and Michael Bolton music.

Matt: Believe me. No candle light. No Michael Bolton music. I felt
like Jane Goodall.

Rachel: That bad?

Matt: Chimps are sexier. I did learn an important lesson though.

Rachel: What?

Matt: Never eat a pizza smothered in hot peppers then go out and let some guy with a beard eat your ass for an hour. You'll pay for it the next day.

Rachel: Don't want to hear about it!

Matt: And you?

Rachel: Ken and I ordered Malaysian and watched some Robert Fripp special on Bravo.

Matt: Who?

Rachel: He's an excellent guitarist. King Crimson.

Matt: King Crimson? You listen to King Crimson?

Rachel: Yeah.

Matt: Look, let's think about this second book with a really hot team. We'd be in complete control.

A light rises on Martin. Matt and Rachel continue to work.

Martin: Hair's graying. Skin's changing. Fine network of lines crisscrossing my flesh like fabric loosening, stretching away from the bones, decaying. Forty-five. Middle age.

Rachel: It's fuckin' scary sometimes.

Matt: What?

Rachel: Success.

Matt: Success is what we've been working for Rachel. Don't start to get scared of it.

Rachel: I'm not scared of it I'm just scared of it.

A light rises on Yves.

Yves: Sa confiance en soi, j'imagine. *(His confidence I suppose.)* He had the English style confidence that always looks you right in the eye and smiles with absolute sincerity even when they're lying or scared. Impossible de résister. *(Impossible to resist.)*

A light rises on Rex.

Rex: He talked to me like he actually cared what I had to say.

Rachel: It's just—things always get watered down y'know. And what about overexposure? Look what happened to The Punisher. Ghost Rider.

Matt: We're talking a bi-monthly comic not guest appearances in every Marvel title in existence. Besides, our readers aren't fan boys. They're intelligent, well read, open-minded people who enjoy satire and outrageous humour.

Rachel: You're right.

Matt:	I know.
Rachel:	But I am allowed to have doubts from time to time.
Matt:	I know.
Rachel:	We're going to launch another title.
Matt:	I know.
Rachel:	But you wouldn't have done it without my agreeing.
Matt:	I know.
Rachel:	You're a dick.
Matt:	I know.
Martin:	Forty-five.
Rex:	There was the thing with my dad. The thing he used to do. When I was sleeping. At night. When everyone was sleeping.
Yves:	Les hommes. On est tous fuckés par rapport à notre père. *(Men. We are all fucked up about our fathers.)*

Lights on Martin, Rex and Yves fade.

Matt:	You really listen to King Crimson?
Rachel:	Why does that surprise you so much?
Matt:	Well I know everything about you and I didn't know that.
Rachel:	You don't know everything about me.
Matt:	Practically everything since grade eleven.
Rachel:	No one knows everything about someone. People always surprise each other.
Matt:	When did I ever surprise you?
Rachel:	When you told me you were gay after you'd been married for two years.
Matt:	Yeah—well other than that?
Rachel:	Knowing everything about someone would make them pretty boring Matt.
Matt:	But isn't that what getting involved with someone's all about? Trying to learn everything about them?
Rachel:	Trying. Not necessarily succeeding.
Matt:	I think it'd be great to know everything about someone.
Rachel:	There's gotta be some mystery pal, or it just doesn't work. I need a toke. Where the hell is Billy?
Matt:	You okay?
Rachel:	Ken.

Matt: Boyfriend trouble.

Rachel: Last night.

Matt: Yeah?

Rachel: When we were laying in bed. He wrote I love you on my back with his finger.

Matt: That bitch.

Rachel: I don't know what to do.

Matt: Are you expected to write I love you on his back with your finger as well?

Rachel: Something like that.

Matt: But you're not ready to write I love you on his back with your finger.

Rachel: I don't think so.

Matt: Perhaps you could write I really really like you on his back with your finger.

Rachel: I think I'm going to write I can't see you anymore on his back with my finger.

Matt: Really?

Rachel: *Nods.* I really don't feel up to having people write I love you on my back with their finger right now.

Matt: I'd really like to have someone write I love you on my back with their finger.

Rachel: You always meet guys.

Matt: Kids in their twenties.

Rachel: What's the bad part?

Matt: I want to spend time with someone who gets my jokes and doesn't understand the metric system.

Rachel: Is this an issue?

Matt: The young ones all think they want to settle down until they settle down. I need to meet a legitimate older gentleman.

Rachel: How would that be different?

Matt: I think it might stick with someone my own age or older. Other than that torrid gay affair I had when I was married I've never had a relationship that's lasted over three months. It's like a curse in the gay community. Three months and it's over. Come to think of it, that thing when I was married was three months too. Jesus.

Rachel: Was there anything in our childhoods that prepared us to be alone so much?

Matt: Television.

The doorbell rings.

Rachel: Bout fuckin' time.

Matt moves to the door and opens it.

Matt: Billy.

Yves: I am Yves.

Matt: What happened to Billy?

Rachel: I'm Rachel.

Yves enters. Matt closes the door. Yves carries a backpack.

Yves: Hi. Billy moved back to Guelph for school. I am the new courier. Same pager number. Nice studio.

Rachel: Thanks.

Matt: From Montreal?

Yves: You can tell so easy?

Matt: You have a Montreal look.

Yves: And what is a Montreal look?

Matt: Relaxed. Sexy.

Yves: Merci. And what is a Toronto look?

Rachel: Constipated.

Yves: I like you two. You are not from Toronto.

Matt: Prince Edward Island via Calgary.

Yves: You too Rachel?

Rachel: P.E.I. without the Calgary part.

Yves: I thought so.

Rachel: Why?

Yves: You are too friendly to be from here.

Matt: There are a million stories in the naked city.

Rachel: But this is Toronto so they're all the same.

Yves: *Laughs.* Yes!

Matt: What've you got today Yves?

Yves opens his backpack and takes out a number of plastic bags, displaying the goods for Matt and Rachel.

Yves: Red hair. Hash. Acid. Ecstasy.

Matt: Real ecstasy or that speedy shit they sell the rave babies?

Yves: The speedy shit they sell the rave babies.

Rachel: Half an ounce of the red hair.

Yves: One hundred and sixty dollars please.

Matt hands Yves money.

Matt: There you go.

Yves takes the money then notices the drawings. He moves to the drawing boards, excited.

Yves: *Suddenly.* SpumBoy and Fridge Magnet Girl?!

Matt: Yeah.

Yves: You are the people who do SpumBoy and Fridge Magnet Girl?

Rachel: That's us.

Yves: Let me shake your hands. Both of you. I love your comic book. It is so funny.

He shakes their hands enthusiastically.

Matt: Thanks.

Yves: You draw this here?

Rachel: We both plot it then Matt does the pencils and dialogue and I draw the backgrounds and ink it.

Yves: I loved the issue where they fought BitchTits the Juice Pig. Very funny.

Matt: I patterned BitchTits after a stripper at Remingtons.

Yves: Not Phil Uranus?

Matt: Yes!

Yves: I knew it. I saw the—uh—resemblance!

Matt: You go to Remingtons?

Rachel: That male strip bar?

Yves: Oh yes. Sometimes Mondays for Spermarama.

Rachel: Spermarama?

Matt: Some of the guys get paid extra to jerk off.

Rachel: Until they come?

Matt: It's the Nineties Rachel.

Rachel: Cool.

Yves: These are the original pages for next issue?

Matt: Right.

Yves: So you are both gay?

Matt: I am.

Rachel: I'm not.

Yves: I see.

Matt: Rachel and I have been friends since high school.

Rachel: We were both comic nerds who hated everyone else.

Matt: Little has changed.

Rachel: Lots has changed.

Sound of Yves's pager beeping.

Yves: Another delivery.

Matt: Thanks for stopping by.

Yves: To meet the creators of SpumBoy and Fridge Magnet girl? The pleasure was all mine. Call anytime.

Yves exits.

Rachel: Nice kid.

Matt: Do you remember any of the French you took in school?

Rachel: Je m'appelle Rachel. (*My name is Rachel.*)

Matt: Anything else?

Rachel: No. I think he likes you.

Matt: He's French. They cruise everyone.

Rachel: He's cute.

Matt: He's a drug dealer.

Rachel: Right.

Matt: What's say we get high and start next month's adventure?

Rachel: Sounds good.

Sound of a streetcar passing outside of Martin's condo.

Matt: You roll.

Yves enters the condo drinking a beer.

Yves: I met somebody very special today.

Rachel: I always roll.

Martin: Who's that?

Yves: The man and woman who created SpumBoy and Fridge Magnet Girl.

Martin: Who?

Yves: You have never heard of SpumBoy and Fridge Magnet Girl?

Martin: I don't know what you're talking about.

Yves: They are comic book heroes. Very funny. SpumBoy can turn anything into processed meat and Fridge Magnet Girl has millions of fridge magnets attached to her body that she controls mentally.

Martin: *Laughs.* That is the most ridiculous thing I've ever heard.

Yves: Yes. It is wonderful. The guy is gay. Kind of cute.

Martin: Really?

Yves: Oui.

Martin: How's the new job?

Yves: Much bicycle riding for not enough money.

Martin: You be careful.

Yves: Careful?

Martin: You don't want to get in some accident with a knapsack filled with drugs.

Yves: Do not worry.

Martin: I can't help it. You know that.

Yves: I will be careful father.

Martin: How are you feeling?

Short pause.

Yves: Fine.

Martin: Just asking.

Yves: Why wouldn't I be?

Martin: They changed your cocktail again.

Yves: And there are no side effects. I am fine.

Martin: No kidney problems from the Crixivan?

Yves: Not so far.

Martin: Good.

Yves: Where is Rex?

Martin: Who knows?

Yves: Tell him I want my money.

Martin: You tell him.

Yves: Has he been blowing his nose a lot lately?

Martin: What's that supposed to mean?

Yves: He was at Woodys talking with Edgar last night.

Martin: Talking to Edgar doesn't mean he's doing coke.

Yves: I do not know any other reason someone talks to Edgar.

Martin: He's not using again.

Yves: Whatever.

Yves moves to Martin and touches him affectionately.

Yves: I need the car tonight.

Martin: Why?

Yves: I promised some queens I'd drive them to the show at Power.

Martin: I don't want you driving when you've been drinking.

Yves: I am not drinking tonight.

Martin: Why don't I drive you?

Yves: I do not want you to drive me.

Martin: Maybe I'll come meet you after the show. That way you don't have to worry about getting it back before I go to work.

Yves: If you like.

Martin: I haven't been out in a while.

Yves: Okay.

Martin: I'll TTC down before last call.

Yves: Pis j'ai besoin d'argent aussi. *(I need some money too.)*

Martin: Je n'ai pas d'argent. *(I don't have any money.)*

Yves: Juste cinquante dollars. *(Just fifty dollars.)*

Martin: Je ne les ai pas. *(I don't have it.)*

Matt and Rachel working in the studio.

Matt: What time is it?

Yves: I need fifty dollars Martin.

Rachel: Just after eleven.

Martin: I'll get it for you after dinner.

Matt: I'm beat.

Rachel: Going out?

Matt: I guess. It's a solo tour tonight.

Rachel: Where's Cam?

Matt: Cam's sick with something.

Rachel: What?

Matt: They're changing his combination again. Every possible side effect these things can give you he gets. Some kidney thing. He's reacting to the Crixivan.

Rachel: The what?

Matt: One of those new protease inhibitors.

Rachel: Why don't I take you for a drink?

Matt: I can never stay awake at straight bars.

Rachel: I have a good time with you no matter where we are.

Matt: You want to come to Power?

Rachel: It's too frustrating. All those gorgeous sensitive guys and I might as well be invisible.

Matt: There'll be men dancing with hardly any clothes on.

Rachel: One drink—and that's it.

Matt: Alright Rachel!

The condo. Rex is taking a shower. He sings to himself. The water is turned off just as Martin opens the door and enters the bathroom.

Rex: You ever hear of fuckin' knocking?

Martin: It is my house.

Rex: Where were you?

Martin: The community centre. We had a rent control meeting.

Rex: Hand me a towel.

Martin hands Rex a towel. Rex dries himself. Martin watches him.

Martin: Going out?

Rex: Thought I might.

Martin: Where to?

Rex: Haven't decided yet. Great tie.

Martin: The salesman said the colour brought out my eyes.

Rex: Looks good.

Martin: Your back's still wet.

Rex tosses Martin the towel.

Rex: Help yourself.

Martin dries Rex's back as they speak.

Martin: Who're you going out with?

Rex: TeeJay.

Martin: Ah.

Rex: She's got some wicked hash. Crazy shit.

Martin: I thought you might like to meet Yves with me.

Rex: Nope.

Martin's hand has moved down so he is now drying Rex's ass. Rex gives him a playful look.

Rex: I hate shaving with a hard on.

Pause. Rex moves away from Martin.

Rex: You got any clean razor blades?

Martin: The second drawer.

Rex opens the drawer and takes the towel from Martin.

Rex: Got a fucking job today.

Martin: Where?

Rex wraps the towel around his waist and rummages through the drawer, finding new blades.

Rex: Some used record shop in the Annex. It's only part time.

Martin: Good for you.

Rex: I'm hoping to have enough for my own place by the end of the month.

Martin: Whenever you're ready. I don't mind having you here.

Rex: I appreciate having a place to stay.

Martin: As long as you follow the rules.

Rex: Yessir.

Martin: Yves said he saw you with Edgar last night.

Rex: Yves just can't wait to tell on me, can he?

Martin: We're just concerned.

Rex: I wasn't buying blow.

Martin: I'd just hate to see you get in trouble again.

Rex: Can you lend me some dough until I get paid?

Martin: You already owe me quite a bit of money Rex.

Rex: Hey dad, I'm good for it.

Martin: I'm not sure how much cash I've got on me.

Rex: You know I'll let you collect for it.

Martin: I'll see what I can do.

Rex: Kewl.

Rick Astley's "Together Forever" blasts into the foreground.
Matt and Rachel have arrived at the club and are carrying beers.
Whooping and cheering men are heard in the background.
Everyone has to yell over the pounding music.

Matt: Oh God. Rick Astley's back?

Rachel: Who?

Matt: Never mind.

Rachel: This place's packed.

Matt: After twelve hours writing and drawing I really need someplace like this.

Rachel: What are those guys snorting over there?

Matt: Special K.

Rachel: The cereal?

Matt: The drug.

Rachel: What is it?

Matt: Cat tranquilizer.

Rachel: What does it do?

Matt: Makes you feel like a tranquilized cat.

Rachel: That explains so much.

Matt sees Yves and Martin across the bar and waves at them.

Matt: Hey, there's buddy from this afternoon.

Rachel: *Waves to Yves.* Yep.

Matt: Oh God.

Rachel: What?

Matt: The guy with him.

Rachel: Yeah?

Matt: He's only like the most attractive guy ever. Politician.

Rachel: He doesn't dress like a politician.

Matt: He dresses like a twelve-year-old. But only at the bars. Don't judge him on it. Most gay men go through at least two adolescences. One fucked up, one fun.

Rachel: Which one would he be in?

Matt: Hard to say.

Yves and Martin join Matt and Rachel.

Yves: Hi.

Matt: Hi Yves.

Rachel: Hey.

Yves: I did not know you came here.

Matt: I don't usually.

Rachel: And I don't ever.

Yves: Have you met Martin?

Matt: No.

Yves: These are the comic guys I was telling to you earlier. Matt and Rachel. This is Martin Yesterday.

Matt: Pleased to meet you.

Martin: You too Matt.

Rachel: Hi.

Martin: Yves tells me you're wildly successful.

Matt: We're not doing too badly.

Martin: You work together?

Rachel: Every day.

Martin: Sort of like a marriage.

Rachel: Only fun.

Yves: Did you see the show?

Matt: No, we just got here.

Rachel: I'm not really into men in dresses.

Matt: She thinks its demeaning to women.

Rachel: I think it's ugly.

Martin: But they're not really trying to be women, they're trying to be men pretending to be women.

Matt: And only a very few are even successful at that.

Martin: It can be offensive at times.

Rachel: And rarely ever pretty.

Yves: I am going to dance.

Martin: Sure.

Yves leaves.

Rachel: *To Martin.* So you're in politics.

Matt: He's the councillor for this very neighbourhood.

Martin: That's right.

Matt: It's not easy to be an out politician.

Martin: It's not easy being an out anything.

Rachel: I read an article that said people are actually more likely to vote for an out gay politician than a straight one because they think the out person has more integrity.

Martin: We're just people like everyone else.

Rachel: That's what I thought when I read the article.

Martin: I need another mineral water. Do either of you want anything?

Matt: I'll have another light beer.

Martin: Sure. Rachel?

Rachel: I'm fine. Thanks.

Martin: Right back. Don't go anywhere.

Matt: Promise.

Martin leaves for more drinks.

Rachel: A politician?!

Matt: Yes. But he uses his political power for good not evil.

Rachel: I've never heard of an honest politician.

Matt: He's different.

Rachel: He's at least forty-something.

Matt: *Thrilled.* At least.

Rachel: I think I should leave you two alone.

Matt: Would you mind?

Rachel: I feel like a tourist here anyway.

Martin returns with beers.

Martin: Here you go.

Matt: Thanks.

Martin: Rachel, would you like to dance?

Rachel: Actually no. I'm sweating like a pig. Very charming of you to ask though. I'm gonna run. Nice to meet you Martin.

Martin: You too Rachel.

Matt: Later.

Rachel leaves.

Martin: She's great.

Matt: Yeah.

Martin: Centred.

Matt: Yes.

An uncomfortable pause filled by the thumping music from the dance floor.

Martin: I'll have to make a point of picking your comic up. Yves says it's very funny.

Matt: I could get you some copies. I've got tons.

Martin: That'd be great. Why don't I give you my card?

Matt: I could get you the comics and we could maybe have dinner or something.

Martin doesn't really hear what Matt has said because of the music. He nods and smiles then realizes Matt said something important.

Martin: What?

Matt: I could get you the comics and we could have dinner.

Martin: I'd like that.

Matt: So would I.

Martin: Great. I'm going to join Yves on the dance floor. It was very nice to meet you Matt. I look forward to hearing from you.

Rachel: So?

Matt: Me too.

Rachel: How was it?

The studio. Day. Rachel's working. Matt joins her. He paces as he speaks, glancing at the telephone from time to time.

Matt: I don't know what it is. Past life connections. Pheromones. Some sort of completely physical reptilian brain response that makes no sense and can't be fought. It made me feel good to talk to him, it made me feel good to look at him. It made me feel good to be near him.

Rachel: Sounds scary.

Matt: I feel like I have no power. Did you like him?

Rachel: A lot. Beware.

Matt: Why?

Rachel: It's the men you like who hurt you the most.

Matt: Don't be cynical when I'm being infatuated.

Sudden sound of a jackhammer on the street, quite loud.

Matt: What the hell is that?

Rachel: Didn't you see the notice at the bottom of the stairs?

Matt: No.

Rachel: Mandatory sewer upgrade. The city apologizes for any inconvenience and hopes to have the work completed within a week or two.

Matt: Fabulash.

Rachel: So did you and Mr. Reptilian Brain Response sleep together?

Matt: No.

Rachel: Why not?

Matt: Thought I'd hold out for a date.

Rachel: Is that why you keep staring at the phone?

Matt: I left this number on his answering machine this morning.

Rachel: You're actually nervous.

Matt: This is Toronto. No one ever calls when they say they will.

Rachel: Maybe the politician will be different.

The telephone rings.

Rachel: Calm down.

Matt checks the call display.

Matt: It's him.

Panicked, Matt throws the phone to Rachel who immediately tosses it back to him. Matt activates the telephone.

Matt: Hi Martin. Yeah. Call display. How are you? Good. Good. Yeah, that'd be great. Okay. See you then. Bye.

Matt throws the phone to Rachel, who hangs it up.

Matt: We're going out tonight.

Rachel: Excited?

Matt: Moist.

The doorbell rings.

Rachel: Pot.

Matt opens the door. Yves is there.

Matt: Salut Yves. *(Hi Yves.)*

Yves: Salut. Ça va? *(Hi. How are you?)*

Matt: Je suis fatigué. Et toi? *(I am tired. And you?)*

Yves: Bien merci. *(Good thanks.)* I did not know you spoke French.

Matt: I'm one of those new kind of Canadians that know a useless smattering of French. Sort of a—francophonette.

Yves: Do you speak French Rachel?

Rachel: No.

Matt: *Quickly.* Forgive her! Don't break up the country because she doesn't speak French!

Yves: Do not worry. I am no separatist.

Matt: I was joking. I figured if you were a separatist you wouldn't be living in Toronto.

Rachel: Unless he's a separatist spy.

Matt: A separatist spy. Infiltrating English Canada to see how the rest of the country feels about Quebec. There's a character idea.

Rachel: Put it on the bulletin board.

Matt: Right beside the Freddy Prinz reincarnation idea.

Yves moves to examine the pages they're working on.

Yves: Oh, I like her. She is very funny.

Matt: Chumpchawalla Lipschitz. She's this rich New York heiress who pretends to be a villain to meet Fridge Magnet Girl.

Yves: I thought Fridge Magnet Girl was straight.

Rachel: So did she.

Matt: Until she met Chumpchawalla. This story arc's gonna be a heartbreaker.

Rachel: It's really only a phase though.

Yves: You want another half ounce?

Rachel: That'd be it.

Yves takes pot out of his knapsack.

Matt: The money's on the light table.

Yves: Merci. You know, I trained as a commercial artist.

Matt: Really?

Yves: At Concordia. I got a scholarship in high school because I was the best art student in St. Henri. I never finished. Too much talking.

Matt: Bring your stuff in some time. We'll take a look at it.

Yves: That would be great.

Rachel: Ahem.

Matt: We're going need an assistant at some point.

Sound of Yves's beeper.

Yves: *Tired.* Shit. Another delivery.

Rachel: Hey, you should be happy for the business.

Yves: I hate riding this stupid bike all over the city. Have fun at *Tommy* tonight.

Matt: How did you know that?

Yves: Martin tells me everything.

Matt: But he just called.

Yves: I knew he had the tickets.

Matt: I didn't realize you were that close?

Yves: Martin and I were lovers for six years.

Pause.

Matt: I didn't know that.

Yves: Oh yes.

Short pause.

Yves: I have to run.

Rachel: Later.

Yves exits.

Matt: Lovers?

Rachel: *Tommy?*

Martin is dressing to go out. Rex lies on the bed, rolling a joint.

Rex: *Tommy?*

Martin: Yes.

Rex: By The How?

Martin: The Who.

Rex: The what?

Martin: The Who.

Rex: Whatever.

Martin: How was work?

Rex: Like being dead only you have to talk. Is this like a date?

Martin: Yes. I guess it's a date.

Rex: You usta take me on dates.

Martin: You used to like them.

Rex: *Shrugs.* Never knew anything like that before.

Martin: It was nice.

Rex: Good shirt.

Martin: Thank you.

Rex: I thought you had no money.

Martin: The tickets were freebies.

Rex: So what makes this guy so hot?

Martin: He is the author of one of the best selling comic books of the Nineties.

Rex: No way.

Martin: SpumBoy and Fridge Magnet Girl.

Rex: Wicked! You're going out with that guy?

Martin: I'm going to dinner with that guy.

Rex: He must be so loaded.

Martin: He's a nice kid.

Rex: You hot for him?

Martin: I'm not not hot for him.

Rex: Right.

Martin: What are you doing?

Rex: TeeJay.

Martin: Have a good time.

Sound of the jackhammer. Loud. The studio.

Rex:	Is he gonna stay here tonight?
Martin:	I don't know. Why?
Matt:	That's going to drive me nuts.
Rex:	Just wonderin'.
Rachel:	You'll get used to it.
Martin:	Jealous?
Matt:	You do not get used to the sound of an intermittent jackhammer.
Rex:	*Very sarcastic.* Yeah right.
Rachel:	You get used to anything eventually.
Matt:	I've gotta stop. My hand is cramping.
Rachel:	I'm gonna finish this page then head.
Matt:	Something on your mind?
Pause.	
Rachel:	You shouldn't do shit like you did with Yves before.
Matt:	What?
Rachel:	Announcing that we're going to need an assistant before we've even talked about it.
Matt:	It just occurred to me at that moment.
Rachel:	It puts me in a weird position.
Matt:	But we do need an assistant.
Rachel:	Then we should talk about it alone first.
Matt:	Right.
Pause.	
Matt:	Seeing Ken tonight?
Rachel:	I'm supposed to.
Matt:	Have you spoken to him since the back writing incident?
Rachel:	On the phone. It's not exactly like I've had time to see anyone with all these deadlines.
Matt:	That reminds me, we have to proof the lettering for the first issue of the second book tomorrow.
Rachel:	We can't keep going at this pace.
Matt:	We could if we had an assistant.
Rachel:	He's your boyfriend's ex-lover.
Matt:	Martin's not my boyfriend.
Rachel:	Not yet. Next time we call Yves we'll ask him to bring his portfolio.

Matt:	Someone to organize the proofs, answer the fan mail, maybe do some secondary inking if necessary.
Rachel:	Only if necessary.
Matt:	What does it mean when you hate facing the fact that the person you're currently interested in had lovers before you came along?
Rachel:	You're nervous, aren't you?
Matt:	I admit it! I'm nervous!
Rachel:	I'll roll a joint.
Matt:	I hate relationships.
Rachel:	Remain calm.
Matt:	They make life so unbearable.

People can be heard talking quietly in the background. Matt and Martin move into theatre seats, whispering to each other.

Rachel:	Do not panic.
Martin:	I'm really looking forward to this.
Rachel:	Take deep breaths.
Matt:	I didn't know you and Yves used to be lovers.
Rachel:	Relax.
Martin:	There are a lot of things you don't know about me.
Matt:	How long ago did you break up?
Martin:	About four years or so. It's hard to keep track.
Matt:	On again off again?
Martin:	Definitely off now.
Matt:	See a lot of each other?
Martin:	He's family. What about you? Any ex-lovers I should know about?
Matt:	Well actually I am the subject of a group of paintings that caused a bit of a stir in Calgary a few years ago.
Martin:	What was it called?
Matt:	Ironically enough—Straight Man.
Martin:	The David McMillan show. That was you?
Matt:	Yep.
Martin:	How's that?
Matt:	Fine except everyone in Canada saw me nude, it destroyed my marriage and I was forced to come out.
Martin:	And look where it's brought you.

Matt: *Tommy* at the Elgin with my local alderman. The heights are dizzying.

Martin: I was talking about the comic book.

Matt: Oh.

Martin: I liked it very much.

Matt: Thanks.

Martin: Hilarious and painful at once.

Matt: Do you always say the absolute right thing?

Martin: It's my job.

Matt: Of course.

Martin: There's something else you should probably know.

Matt: What?

Martin: I live with a twenty-three year old boy.

Matt: Oh.

A moment from the overture of Tommy *swells as the lights change. Sound of Yonge Street at eleven o'clock on a Saturday night. Matt and Martin rise and walk.*

Martin: His name's Rex. He's an ex-lover as well.

Matt: And you live with him?

Martin: He's been having some personal trouble and needs a place to stay.

Matt: Right.

Martin: He's had some trouble with his father.

Matt: So you replaced the father.

Martin: I like taking care of people.

Matt: Y'know Martin, I'm starting to notice this theme with your exes. Young.

Martin: I admit I've had some problems with younger guys.

Matt: Problems?

Martin: The usual—stolen stereo equipment, carelessly broken heart. They've been a bit of a drug. It's—they're—I'm trying to change things.

Matt: Me too.

Martin: Matt, I didn't come out or have sex until I was thirty-five. I've always had this real thing for the years I missed. Truthfully it hasn't always been very healthy. I really am trying to get a handle on it.

A distant siren is heard approaching.

Matt:	Thirty-five? You had no sexual feelings at all?
Martin:	Not ones I could recognize.
Matt:	Must've been very frustrating.
Martin:	Yes. I should've dealt with it sooner. It was a mistake to avoid it for so long. But I really wasn't sure what the problem was.
Matt:	So you were celibate.
Martin:	A virgin until a young guy practically held me down and blew me in the sauna at the pool one day.
Matt:	That was the point you realized you were gay?
Martin:	It's pretty hard to deny it when a man has his mouth wrapped around your cock and you can't stop crying.
Matt:	Crying?
Martin:	I couldn't help it. It was the most wonderful horrible thing I'd ever experienced.
Matt:	I sort of know exactly what you mean. You must've been very good at lying to yourself.
Martin:	Yes. You were a late bloomer as well.
Matt:	At least I was having sex with someone. Even if it was someone I wasn't truly attracted to.
Martin:	You never found your wife attractive?
Matt:	I did. But I found men more attractive.
Martin:	So you've spent some time lying to yourself as well.
Matt:	Oh yeah.

The siren sound peaks as it roars by then quickly recedes.

Martin:	I had a very nice time.
Matt:	Me too.
Martin:	Should we go out again?
Matt:	I'd like that.
Martin:	I've decided I want to sleep with you.
Matt:	I'm honoured.
Martin:	But not yet.
Matt:	No?
Martin:	I like to give things time.
Matt:	I'm into that.
Martin:	Good.

The studio. Matt joins Rachel, who is working.

Matt: How's Ken?

Rachel: Rather heartbroken today I'd think.

Matt: You did it?

Rachel: Do you have any idea how hard it is to write I can't see you anymore on someone's back with your finger?

Matt: No I'm the one who always gets dumped remember? Is this an issue?

Rachel: I feel shitty but I'm fine.

Matt: We didn't have sex.

Rachel: Was it a good time?

Matt: He seems to like younger guys.

Rachel: I think you're trying to talk yourself out of this before it even starts.

Matt: It's a guaranteed way to keep from being hurt.

Rachel: Saves a break-up later on.

Matt: Why'd you dump Ken?

Rachel: He liked me far more than he should have for the amount he knew me.

Matt: Always makes me suspicious.

Rachel: Besides...

Matt: What?

Rachel: He wanted me to bite him.

Matt: Bite him?

Rachel: When he was about to come. Hard.

Matt: But Ken's a lawyer.

Rachel: I suspect those two things are closely connected.

Matt: Eew.

Rachel: What is it with you men? Every one of you seems to want some specialized service. The guy I went out with before Ken wanted to spank me and the guy before that was really only into anal sex. Anyway, I shouldn't complain. One of The Girls is seeing a guy who fucks her high heels.

Matt: How does she get off?

Rachel: I didn't think to ask.

Matt: Whatever gets you through the night.

Rachel: Sometimes I think pornography has damaged all the men of my generation. It's hard maintaining relationships with sex freaks.

Matt: You know, it's not just about meeting the right person, it's also meeting the right person at the right time.

Yves: You should see the guy I met last night.

Martin's condo. Martin is working at his laptop. Yves is helping himself to food in the fridge.

Rachel: The world's too complicated for love.

Yves: At the Barracks. He was so hot. Meaty. Arms like hams and so hairy.

Matt: Write that down.

Martin: Aren't you working today?

Yves: I took the day off.

Martin: Is that such a good idea?

Yves: *Shrugs.* Someone will cover for me. Martin, are you seeing Matt soon?

Martin: Tomorrow night.

Yves: You like him.

Martin: I do. He's—abrasively stimulating.

Yves: Focused.

Martin: That's a good word.

Yves: I would like you to talk to him about me.

Martin: Why?

Yves: I have been working on some drawing—uh—demonstrations?

Martin: Samples.

Yves: Oui. Samples. And he said he would look at them. I thought it might help even more if you talked to him about me. If you—uh—*searches for the right word*—uh—

Martin: Promoted?

Yves: Oui. Promoted me some.

Martin: Why should I do that?

Yves: Because if you talk to him about me I will not talk to him about you.

Pause.

Martin: If there's an opportunity I'll say something.

Yves: Trouve-la l'opportunité, Martin. *(Make one Martin.)*

Rex enters, looking burnt out and tired.

Martin: Are you just getting in?

Rex: Yeah.

Martin: You okay?

Rex: Fine. Hey Yves.

Yves: Salut. Do you have my eighty dollars?

Rex: Shit no man. I've got no fucking money.

Yves: It has been two months.

Rex: I haven't been paid yet.

Martin: And where have you been all night?

Rex: TeeJay and I did some ecstasy. I think it was speed though. Didn't sleep all fucking night.

Yves: Any coke?

Rex: I'm clean Yves.

Martin: You look very pale.

Rex: I'm okay. Is that a new sweater?

Martin: Please—I've had this thing for years.

Rex: I'm gonna crash for a while. Don't wake me up, okay.

Martin: 'night.

Rex exits to his bedroom.

Yves: He is just using you.

Martin: Rex needs a safe place to stay.

Yves: Rex needs a free place to stay.

Martin turns off his laptop and stands, getting ready to leave.

Martin: I've got to speak to the Yonge Street Reclamation League. We're trying to get sandwich boards banned from the sidewalks.

Yves: J'ai besoin de quarante dollars. *(I need forty dollars.)*

Martin: For what?

Yves: Cat food and litter.

Martin reaches into his pocket and hands Yves two twenties.

Martin: And that's it.

Yves: Martin, my phone bill is overdue as well. And the super is talking about raising the rent on my bachelor.

Martin: I don't have time to deal with this now Yves.

Rachel: Is this a person or a protoplasmic blob or what?

Yves: You will always have time for me Martin.

Matt: Where?

Martin: Are you sure of that Yves?

Rachel: Behind SpumBoy.

Yves: Oui.

The studio. Matt and Rachel are working.

Matt: It could be a shopping cart.

Rachel: I can't ink it if I don't know what it is.

Matt: Make it a dog.

Rachel: I'm gonna make it a garbage can.

Matt: But I want a surprised dog.

Rachel: If you're not gonna draw it clearly you get whatever I draw fastest.

Matt: Are you looking for a fight?

Rachel: No. I'm looking for a fucking break. I've been inking for fifteen hours and I'm still two pages behind. Fuck!

Matt: Relax. Roll a joint. We'll take a break.

Rachel: I need to stretch. You roll.

Matt: Let's cut straight to the assistant issue. Yves.

Rachel: We're still at least a week behind.

Matt: No problem. We'll run the Frank Miller inventory story.

Rachel: Fans hate fill-in issues.

Matt: Maybe we'll even do our first glow in the dark, prismafoilamatic wraparound cover.

Rachel: Fill-in!

Matt: Yes, Rachel! It is a fill-in. But it will be a beautiful fill-in. And we'll make a fortune from it.

Matt produces a joint.

Rachel: Should I light this joint?

Matt: Hugh Betcha!

Rachel: You're in a good mood all of a sudden.

Matt: Martin and I are going to Canada's Wonderland tonight. Then out for dinner then WE'RE GOING TO SLEEP TOGETHER. I think. He's asked me to stay at his place and I accepted. Hopefully he's not gonna put me in the guest room.

Rachel: Excited?

Matt: Trembling like a schoolgirl.

Rachel: What's to be scared of?

Matt: The very telling suspicion that he's too intimidatingly handsome for someone like me.

Rachel: Matt, you're a fine looking man.

Matt: Not in the gay community. We've become a society of body Nazis. Love handles have become the leprosy of the Nineties.

Rachel: This guy likes you.

Matt: Yeah?

Rachel: I can tell. So why don't you trust that and let someone like you for a change?

Matt: What exactly does that mean?

Rachel: It means I think you sometimes push people away because you're afraid they're going to reject you.

Matt: But they *are* going to reject me.

Rachel: We've all had shitty relationships pal.

Matt: This one's gonna be different. I'm gonna take my time. No pressure. Let things develop. What are you doing with your day off?

Rachel: Lunch with The Girls. I haven't seen them for ages and they always make me feel better after a breakup.

Matt: But you were the breaker-upper.

Rachel: One still feels bad.

Matt: It's so gratifying to hear that. Say hi to The Girls for me.

Rachel: I will.

Calliope music and sudden terrified loud screams from people on a roller coaster.

Martin: Toronto was getting so big and I'd just come out and was doing some volunteer work with the Coalition for Equal Families. I somehow became the media liaison for them— mostly because no one else wanted to do it—which led to a lot of commenting on issues for the media which led to a certain public recognition factor which led to running for office on a dare practically and actually winning. Ten years later I'm still here.

Matt: Do any of your fellow aldermen have problems with your sexuality?

Martin: Less than you think.

In the distance a woman shrieks with delight.

Martin: Some of them don't understand it but they keep it to themselves. They're a fairly well educated group. A lot of my constituents are straight too. I've got the whole Dundas

Parliament area. I spend more time listening to people bitch about the hookers than I do listening to gay concerns.

Matt: Why do you do it?

Martin: It's very important to me that Toronto be a really terrific place to live.

Matt: And is it?

Martin: It's getting better all the time.

Matt: I occasionally find Toronto self-consciously shallow.

Martin: It used to be worse. There was a time they kept women, drag queens and punk rockers out of the gay clubs here. If that's what the gay community was like try to imagine the straight community of the time.

Matt: Sometimes I feel like Toronto's still like that. It's just better at hiding it now.

Martin: I've read some of the interviews you've done. That little profile of you and Rachel in *Maclean's* was interesting.

Matt: Interesting?

Martin: You seem harder in the media.

Matt: So do you.

Martin: They seem to talk about you a lot more than Rachel.

Matt: I know. She doesn't say anything but I know it bothers her. Her work is as important as mine, but because I'm the writer slash penciller people think I'm the one doing all the work. There've been some studios and production companies sniffing around the book lately. They all want to talk to me. Rachel doesn't even occur to them.

Martin: It's difficult, having a public profile, isn't it?

Matt: The only thing fame ensures is that most everyone you meet will know more about you than you do about them.

Martin: *Laughs.* It's not easy being a role model.

Matt: I don't know what kinda role model I am. I just try to be honest.

Martin: You do a very good job.

Matt: So do you.

Martin puts his arm around Matt's shoulders affectionately.

Martin: Are you aware Yves draws?

Matt: You think I should hire him?

Martin: *Shrugs.* That's your decision.

Matt: You wouldn't have a problem with it?

Pause.

Martin: Well—there's plenty of potential for possible conflict, but we're all adults and Yves needs the work.

Matt: Rachel and I have already discussed it.

Martin: Really?

Matt: I'm calling him Monday.

The roller coaster sound has grown progressively louder.

Matt: That is one big roller coaster.

Martin: It's my favorite.

Matt: You want to go on it?

Martin: Yes. Don't you?

Matt: It's awfully big.

Martin: I thought you'd like that.

Matt: I'm actually terrified of roller coasters.

Martin: I'll hold your hand.

Matt: Promise?

They have arrived at the roller coaster and board it. Rotating office chairs work well with rear projection for the roller coaster. It can also be created through sound and lights without video. In either case the actors' movements within the chair are what will ultimately make it convincing.

Martin: Relax. You'll love it.

Matt: Sure I will.

An announcer is heard welcoming the riders. The roller coaster starts. Matt gives a small yell.

Martin: Adrenaline cleans the garbage out of your system.

Matt: Who's gonna clean out my pants?

Martin: You'll be fine.

Matt: I hate it! I hate it!

Martin: *Laughs.* Take my hand. You've got the nicest fingers I've ever seen.

Matt: It's from all the drawing.

Martin: The next one's the big one.

Matt: Oh God.

Martin: You're one of the most honest guys I've ever met.

Matt: Thanks.

Martin: I enjoy our time together very much.

Matt: You're the most interesting person I've met in—in years.

Martin: Scared?

Matt: Am I squeezing your hand too tight?

Martin: I don't mind.

Matt: Good.

Martin: But I've got to tell you—

Matt: What?

Martin: I'm HIV positive.

The cart hits the top of the hill. The crowd screams with sudden, insane laughter as the cart careens down the hill. Matt joins the crowd, screaming lustily. The roller coaster glides to a halt. Matt and Martin disembark.

Martin: I'm okay with it. I saw a therapist. I was going through my mid-life thing as well. I had to reconcile a lot of things anyway.

A strain of strangely haunting calliope music rises from the chaos around them.

Matt: When did you test?

Martin: Two years ago.

Matt: Jesus.

Martin: My doctor thinks I got it from oral sex.

Matt: Really?

Martin: Bleeding gums.

Matt: Can we sit down for a minute?

Martin: Of course. You alright?

Matt sits.

Matt: Sure.

Martin: I'd finally resigned myself to having a fatal disease when they announced the arrival of the protease inhibitors and now we're all—apparently—going to live a lot longer than we expected. My viral load was moderate so my immune system hasn't been damaged too badly.

Matt: Is this an issue?

Martin: There's nothing I can do to change it.

Matt: No.

Martin: In a way, it's the best thing that's ever happened to me.

Matt: What?

Martin: It forced me to get my life and priorities together. I really am okay with it.

Matt: Nearly everyone I know is HIV positive.

Pause.

Martin: Are you?

Matt: No.

Martin: Keep it that way.

Matt: I intend to.

Martin: You still want to sleep with me?

Pause. Matt kisses Martin. It's a long, horny kiss.

Martin: I have a couple hits of ecstasy. We could go to Joy and dance for a while.

Matt: Look, since we're being so honest and out in the open and all I think I should tell you something too.

Martin: What's that?

Short pause.

Matt: I'm on Prozac.

Martin: Do you have a problem with depression?

Matt: No well yeah. Yeah sure. My father was an alcoholic who disappeared one day, my mother was an exotic dancer who put four kids through school on her tips. Of course I have a problem with depression. That's not really why I took it though. I mean we can only use our screwed-up parents as an excuse for our screwed-up lives for so long, right?

Martin: So why are you taking it?

Matt: I've been reading all these articles and there's these television programs and everyone talks about how it helped them become more—braver.

Martin: Braver?

Matt: More confident. More outgoing. All the things we need to succeed. And I want to be like that.

Martin: You want to be American.

Matt: Yeah but nice.

Martin: You seem like that to me.

Matt: No one knows about this. Not even Rachel.

Martin: Your terrible secret is safe with me. Has Prozac been what you're looking for?

Matt: Not particularly. But I've found this in-between place I never knew about. Sort of an in-between not sad not happy place. And I get this odd burning sensation at the back of my brain at around three o'clock everyday. It's not unpleasant though. And there're other side effects—

Martin: Like what?

Matt: I can't come.

Martin: Really?

Matt: Some people lose interest in sex entirely which to my mind makes it clear why they're not depressed anymore. With me the desire's all there, there's just no payoff.

Martin: Then we'll just hold each other and cuddle.

Matt: You're perfect.

Martin: I know.

Matt and Martin kiss, music rises; they are very stoned. They remove one another's clothes as the lights change to suggest Martin's condo. The music crossfades to the sound of the streetcar passing.

Matt: That streetcar run all night?

Martin: Yes. After twenty years I don't even hear it anymore. How are you feeling?

Matt: Terrific.

Martin: Let's take a melatonin each. It'll slow us down.

Matt: Yeah.

Martin gets a bottle and gives each of them a couple of pills.

Matt: You've got an amazing body.

Martin: For a man my age.

Matt: For a man of any age.

They kiss, feeling one another's bodies.

Martin: Your skin's so soft and smooth.

Matt: I've never been this stoned and had sex.

Martin: It's very J.W. King.

Matt: Who?

Martin: He was a porn star. He's dead. Never mind.

They kiss again.

Martin: It's getting chubby.

Matt: Keep that up and it'll get quite fat.

Martin: That sounds tempting.

The door opens suddenly. Rex enters.

Rex: Hey Martin—

Matt and Martin break, surprised.

Rex: *Laughs.* Whoa! Like Bad Timing Boy.

Martin: What can I do for you?

Rex: Hey you're the comic dude right?

Matt: Right.

Martin: This is Rex.

Matt: Hi.

Rex: Let me shake your hand. You're known man.

Matt: Thanks.

Rex shakes Matt's hand.

Rex: Nice dick.

Matt: Thanks!

Martin: What can I do for you?

Rex: Uh—TeeJay's waiting in the car. We're gonna cruise out to Ajax to visit this dude she knows and I need like twenty bucks to gas up the vehicle.

Martin: Are you stoned?

Rex: What?

Martin: Are you stoned?

Rex: No!

Martin: Hand me my pants.

Rex hands Martin his pants. Martin goes through the pockets until he locates a twenty and gives it to Rex.

Martin: And I want it back when you get paid.

Rex: Thanks pop.

Martin: And in the future knock before coming into my room.

Rex: Later, comic dude.

Matt: Nice to meet you.

Rex exits.

Matt: Who's TeeJay?

Martin: His girlfriend.

Matt: You guys still sleep together?

Martin: No.

Matt: Was he stoned?

Martin: I hope not. Rex had quite a coke problem when we first met. He was in rehab for a while. He knows if he starts doing it again he's not welcome to stay here. I want this to be a safe place for him while he's getting his life together. But I'm not going to tolerate any more bullshit.

Matt: I can't believe you live with someone named Rex.

Martin: It's not his real name.

Matt: What's his real name?

Martin: I don't know.

Matt: What?

Martin: He refuses to tell me.

Matt: Rex?

Martin: He thinks it makes him sound like a porn star.

Matt: It makes him sound like a dog. Is Yves going to show up too?

Martin: I wouldn't be surprised. He often does. Especially when he's high and doesn't get lucky.

Matt: You don't mind?

Martin: Not usually. Having Rex around keeps Yves in line. They hate one another.

Matt: That's handy.

Martin stretches out next to Matt.

Martin: I don't want to talk about them.

Matt: *Yawns.* I think the melatonin just kicked in.

Martin puts his arms around Matt.

Martin: I need to sleep.

Matt: Sure.

Pause.

Martin: You feel very good next to me Matt.

Matt: So do you.

Sound of the streetcar passing. Matt is singled out in a spot. Martin makes gradually rising sex sounds in the darkness behind him.

Matt: At some point late the next day I wake up in the darkened, damp smelling bedroom in that sort of gluey still stoned, half awake way you sometimes wake up in after doing drugs and I'm hard between his thighs and he's moving and I'm not sure if I woke him up or he woke me up but somehow we just slide into the sex. It all starts really carefully and gentle but we both know what we really want and before long I'm pulling a condom on and praying my hard on doesn't die like it sometimes does when I'm putting a rubber on and then I'm in him and we're both moaning and the room smells like sweat and bleach and for the first time since I started taking the Prozac I'm glad I can't come because I don't want it to end.

The lights quickly snap to black and immediately rise, very bright. It's morning. Matt and Martin wake.

Martin: What time is it?

Matt: Nearly three.

Martin: Jesus.

Matt: Hung over?

Martin: I'm not too bad. You?

Matt: Fine.

They get out of bed.

Martin: Come on. I'll buy you a very late breakfast.

Matt: I'll buy. You got the drugs.

Martin: They were actually left over from the Rex days.

They dress.

Martin: When I first met Rex I was doing a lot of drugs.

Matt: You don't have like a substance abuse thing do you?

Martin: No more than anyone else. You?

Matt: Pot.

Martin: That's why you know Yves.

Matt: Exactly.

Martin: His health isn't the best.

Matt: Oh?

Martin: They keep changing his cocktail. None of the combinations seem to work right.

Matt: He's HIV positive too?

Martin: Oh yeah. His job record's never been very good. He's a talented boy though.

Rachel: AIDS?

Martin: He has a great imagination.

Rachel: AIDS?

Matt: Lotsa personality.

Matt joins Rachel in the studio.

Rachel: Martin's got AIDS?

Matt: He doesn't have AIDS. He's HIV positive. There's a difference.

Rachel: Matt, he's gonna die.

Matt: Rachel, we're all gonna die.

Rachel: Hopefully not for a while.

A short burst from the jackhammer.

Matt: Anyway AIDS is practically a manageable disease now. It's not a for sure death sentence anymore.

Rachel: You want to end up with the virus?

Matt: We're careful.

Rachel: Women still get pregnant when we use condoms.

Matt: Have you used condoms every time you've had sex since 1981?

Pause.

Matt: We live with this thing every day. You don't understand.

Rachel: Because I'm a woman?

Matt: Because you're straight.

The condo. Yves is there. Martin enters from the bedroom, pulling on his jacket .

Yves: I quit the job today.

Rachel: Right. How could I understand?

Martin: Why?

Matt: It's different for us.

Yves: The bicycle riding is too hard.

Martin: Your legs still bothering you?

Yves: At night I can hardly dance.

Martin: What if Matt doesn't give you the job?

Yves: I'll go back on welfare.

Martin: I didn't give you any money today did I?

Yves: No. Why?

Martin: I thought I had another twenty dollars on me.

Martin moves to exit.

Yves: Where are you off to?

Martin: There's been a murder over on Grosvenor.

Yves: *Excited.* Murder?

Martin: Someone shot a hustler last night. Execution style.

Yves: Really?

Martin: The entire ghetto's in an uproar. Of course, no one in the mainstream cares, except for the sensational bits. I'm going to see if I can at least humanize the victim.

Yves: Where will you be later?

Martin: Matt's then Woodys for a beer.

Yves: Perhaps I will meet you there too.

Martin: You know, I'd prefer if you didn't.

Yves: Oh?

Martin: It's very hard for Matt and I to find time together. I'd like to have him on my own tonight.

Yves: Whatever.

The studio.

Matt: So we hire him?

Rachel: You're sure you want to do this?

Matt: Sure.

Rachel: That creepy guy from that comic fanzine called for you again. He wants to do another interview.

Matt: I'll ignore him for another week.

Rachel: Why don't they ever interview me?

Matt: I don't know.

There's a knock at the door. Martin enters.

Martin: Hey.

Matt and Martin kiss quickly.

Rachel: Hi.

Martin: How are you Rachel?

Rachel: Can't bitch.

Martin: That's a great outfit.

Rachel: Why thank you for saying so.

Martin: Great studio.

Matt: It has its charms.

Martin checks the place out as they speak.

Martin: All this light.

Rachel: Smoke a joint?

Martin: Sure.

Rachel lights a joint.

Matt: What's the story on the murder?

Martin: Sixteen-year-old hustler shot in the middle of the night. No one knows anything. No one saw anything. His parents thought he was in his bed in Scarborough.

Rachel: How horrible.

Martin: We could keep things like this from happening if we had a designated commercial sex area in the city. When is middle-class Toronto going to clue into the fact that prostitution has always existed and always will? Outlawing prostitution just keeps it underground and makes it easier for underage kids from Scarborough to get involved.

Martin hands the joint to Rachel, who almost tokes on it, then changes her mind and passes it to Matt.

Rachel: Is that what you said on television?

Martin: Pretty much.

Rachel: Progressive yet moral. Works for me.

Martin: I'm glad you approve.

Rachel: I bet that you look great on video too.

Rachel's nervousness with the joint is not lost on Matt.

Martin: People have said that. There aren't a lot of women working in comic books are there?

Rachel: Traditionally no. Although there've been a number of great female cartoonists. It's always been male dominated. Comics cater to little boys and their fantasies, not little girls.

The joint is passed around, Rachel always passing it without toking. Martin doesn't notice.

Matt: SpumBoy and Fridge Magnet Girl are meant to appeal to men and women.

Rachel: It's not just muscle guys and chicks with impossibly long legs and tits like watermelons cut in half.

Matt: I personally love drawing chicks with tits like watermelons cut in half.

Rachel: As long as I'm half of this team—no stereotypes.

Matt: They're not stereotypes, they're archetypes.

Rachel: It creates a false ideal.

Matt: The men's tits are as big as the women's.

Martin: Do you really think it's that influential?

Rachel: Little girls see those images and they want to look like that. Little boys see those images and assume they already look like that.

Matt: Well then it's just as damaging to boys.

Rachel: No. It's not.

Martin hands the joint to Rachel who immediately passes it to Matt.

Matt: Not smoking?

Rachel: Too high already.

Martin: What's this?

Rachel: That's the compressor for my airbrush. In case I want to render effects or whatever.

Martin: I didn't realize creativity was so technical.

Rachel: Please. We should be doing half this work on the computer but Mister Technophobe here refuses.

Matt: Computers scare me.

Martin: I wish my office said as much about me as this studio says about you two.

Matt: No you don't. You want people to vote for you.

Martin: Funny. Who's this?

Matt: That's a character sketch for The Deceptive Elf.

Martin: The what?

Rachel: He's this spy from Quebec who's trying to find out how English Canada really feels about Quebeckers.

Martin: And what does he discover?

Matt: That English Canada is terrified of Quebec's unique culture and will do anything they can to eradicate it.

Martin: I don't know if that's very accurate.

Rachel: We're going for satire and conflict.

Matt: And it has some historical validity. *To Martin.* Come on, I need a beer.

Rachel: 'night boys.

Martin: Good night Rachel.

Matt kisses Martin on the mouth quickly, for Rachel's benefit.

Matt: 'night.

Matt and Martin leave the studio. As Matt leaves he pointedly hands Rachel the joint. She takes it from him and watches them leave. She looks at the joint, decides she's being stupid about sharing a joint with someone who's HIV positive, and takes a huge toke.

Woodys. Matt and Martin are there. Music plays. Men are heard around them.

Martin: Do you really think most people want to destroy something that's unique and special?

Matt: Most people fear change and anything that's different. They don't like to see people succeed. They want to keep everyone at their same level of mediocrity. It's safer.

Martin: That I'll agree with.

Matt: Unless people not of the majority demand recognition they never get it. French. Gay. Jewish. Black. Female—although they're not really a minority they're just treated like they are. Old—and they're only a minority for like another year or something. Whatever. Unless you're willing to fight you get nothing.

Martin: Do you know how lucky you are to be able to express an honest and unpopular opinion so candidly Matt?

Matt: I have an idea.

Martin: I admire that about you.

Matt: Thank you.

Pause. Martin kisses Matt.

Martin: I'm glad you enjoy it so much.

Matt: I don't think I could live any other way.

Martin: You mean that, don't you?

Matt: Absolutely. I have to piss. I'll be right back.

Martin: I'll be here.

Matt exits. Martin notices Rex standing in a corner. Martin moves to Rex quickly.

Martin: Did you take twenty dollars out of my wallet?

Rex: What?

Martin: Did you take twenty dollars out of my wallet?

Rex: I didn't want to wake you up.

Martin: You came into my room while I was sleeping?

Rex: You come into my room when I'm sleeping.

Martin: Look Rex, you already owe me quite a lot of money and I haven't seen you with a cheque from this so-called job of yours since you got it.

Rex: So maybe it's time to collect again. It's been a while.

Pause.

Martin: No.

Rex: Really?

Martin: I—don't want to.

Rex: What? The comic dude's a "relationship"?

Pause.

Martin: I'm not interested in anyone else right now.

Rex: Whatever.

Matt joins them.

Matt: Hi.

Rex: Hi. You guys hear about that murder?

Martin: Of course.

Rex: I heard that hooker was shot point blank range, right in his face.

Martin: Back of the head actually.

Rex: Scary man.

Martin: I need a beer. Matt?

Matt: Sure—something light.

Martin: Rex?

Rex: I'll down a quick Ice if you're buying.

Martin leaves.

Rex: You drink light beer?

Matt: It's a Jenny Craig thing. Where's your girlfriend tonight?

Rex: Wherever.

Matt: Slumming at the gay bar?

Rex: Gotta problem with that?

Matt: You have to admit, it is unusual.

Rex: Not to me. Nice shirt.

Matt: Thanks.

Rex: Hey what're the back issues of your comics selling for now?

Matt: Last I heard number one in mint was at a hundred and twenty US.

Rex: Kewl. I hope you hoarded a bunch away.

Matt: We hung onto a few.

Rex: I know a guy right off the top of my head who'd give you two hundred easy for wunna them first issues.

Matt: That so?

Rex: Interested?

Matt: Not particularly. I have a lot of money already. So are you straight or gay?

Rex: I'm whatever's working best at the time.

Matt: You don't find that confusing?

Rex: There's a lotta things I find confusing, but sex isn't one of them.

Matt: So you're bi.

Rex: Those kind of labels are so Eighties.

Matt: Why is it your generation is so much more like that than mine?

Rex: We had better upbringings.

Matt: We're all from dysfunctional families.

Rex: Not me. My family was great.

Matt: Really?

Rex: Why are you so surprised?

Matt: I don't know. I thought Martin said something about trouble with your family.

Rex: No way. My family's the Brady Bunch, dude. Couldn't ask for a nicer group of people.

Short pause.

Matt: How did you end up with Martin?

Rex: He was good to me.

Matt: He's a good guy.

Rex: Yeah.

Pause.

Rex: I think you're the oldest guy he's ever dated.

Matt: You make me feel ancient.

Rex: Ancient's okay.

Matt: Really?

Rex: Sometimes.

Martin returns with beers.

Martin: The buff bartender is apparently simple-minded.

Matt: I was just flirting with your roommate.

Martin: He's quite flirtable. You don't usually hang out at Woodys.

Rex: I'm here to enter the best chest contest.

Martin: What?

Rex: It's a hundred dollars cash prize.

Martin: You know you can't do this while you're living with me.

Rex: I need the dough.

Martin: Rex, you can't enter the best chest contest.

Rex: Why not?

Martin: Because you haven't got a particularly good chest.

The announcer is heard.

Announcer: All contestants for Woodys best chest contest to the centre bar, please.

Rex: Any of you guys interested in some really intense hydroponic weed from Vancouver this guy I know's got?

Matt: When are you seeing this guy?

Rex: Later tonight. Early tomorrow.

Matt: How much?

Rex: Eighty a quarter.

Matt takes money from his wallet and hands it to Rex.

Matt: Get me a half.

Rex: It might take an extra day if the guy's not around.

Matt: Whatever.

Rex: Kewl. I'm gonna blow. Peace.

Rex leaves.

The studio. Rachel is setting up to work. Yves is there.

Rachel: You understand that there's very little actual drawing involved. It's mostly studio upkeep and boring admin shit.

Yves: Oui.

Rachel: Can you start Monday?

Yves: Of course.

There is a sudden blast of the jackhammer.

Rachel: They were supposed to be finished that two weeks ago.

Yves: It is happening everywhere in the city.

Rachel: We'll only need you from noon to six or seven usually.

Yves: Merci. Matt is at the beach with Martin today?

Rachel: How did you know that?

Yves: Martin tells me everything.

Rachel: Really?

Yves: Yes.

Rachel: Everything?

Yves: Oui.

Sound. Seagulls and water lapping at the shore in waves. An occasional, distant dog bark.

Martin: Do you have sunscreen on?

Matt: Of course.

Martin: Don't want to burn that delicate skin.

Matt: I don't usually burn.

Martin: I do. Every year. I figure if I haven't contracted melanoma by now I probably never will.

Matt: Skin cancer is so contemporary. What did you tell them at the office?

Martin: That I had an urgent personal matter that needed immediate attention. How did you squeeze in an afternoon at the beach?

Matt: Drew all night. Where the hell has Rex been?

Martin: He hasn't been home for a few days.

Matt: Guess I can kiss my hundred and sixty bucks good-bye.

Martin: I'm sure he'll get it back to you.

Matt: Why did you break up?

Martin: He wanted to go out with guys closer to his own age and I thought I should too.

Matt: Don't you hate all those complications?

Martin: Rex and I decided we'd still live together but as roommates. We kept doing coke.

Matt: The post breakup coke thing.

Martin: I used it to give myself permission to have unsafe sex.

Matt: Getting fucked without a rubber?

Martin: That's when I tested. Just after Rex and I broke up. Then he got arrested breaking into a home in Rosedale. That's when I sent him to rehab and got off that shit myself. After spending what little money I had and screwing my credit cards up real good.

Matt: Do you still support Rex?

Martin: I'm keeping a tab.

Matt: He told me he was close to his family.

Martin: You'll find his stories change a lot.

Matt: I thought you said you got it from oral sex.

Martin: What?

Matt: HIV. At Wonderland you said you got it from oral sex.

Martin: It really isn't important how I got it.

Matt: I know a lotta people that suck a lotta dick and none of them has tested positive.

Matt stretches out on his stomach.

Martin: Then they're very lucky.

Matt: Why do some of us get it and others don't?

Martin: That's not what I want to talk about.

Martin moves close to Matt and begins to nuzzle him.

Matt: So what do you want to talk about?

Martin: My gradually hardening cock.

Matt: People will see.

Martin: There's no one around.

Martin slides onto Matt's back and kisses his neck. Their bathing suits or shorts are kept on during the following.

Martin: Just you and me and all those seagulls.

Matt: Mmm.

Martin: Enjoying a little lakeside frottage.

Matt: Sounds good.

Martin begins to move against Matt's back.

Martin: Move around some more. Struggle a bit.

Martin holds Matt down, still moving against him. The sky darkens. Distant rumbling of thunder is heard.

Martin: Struggle more. Fight back.

Matt tries to fight back. Martin is moving against his back more urgently.

Martin: Fight. Yeah. Try to stop me. Struggle. Come on. Try to stop me. Fight Matt. Come on. Try to get me off. Fight me.

Martin comes, rubbing himself against Matt. He rolls off Matt quickly. Both are breathing heavily.

Matt: Intense.

The sound of the wind has gradually insinuated itself into the beach ambiance.

Martin: It's clouding up.

Matt: Look at that thunderhead coming across the lake.

Martin: If we don't head back to the car now we're in for a drenching.

There is a sudden, loud crash of thunder. Another clap of thunder, more distant. The studio. A light rises on Rachel, working alone. Yves enters with an umbrella.

Yves: Bonjour.

Rachel: Hola.

Yves: Beautiful day.

Yves shakes out his umbrella.

Rachel: At least the rain keeps the jackhammer people at bay.

Yves: So where shall I start?

Rachel: There's a sack of fan mail over on the desk. Read it and pull the most interesting ones for us.

Matt enters from the bathroom, drying his hands.

Matt: Interesting would be anything thoughtful and considered.

Rachel: We like constructive criticism and people who figure out our pop cult references.

Yves: When do I get to do some artwork?

Matt: When we're caught up on everything else.

Rachel: And behind on the drawing. Yves, I've got those pages packaged up for the courier. I'll leave the packing slip on top if you want to call them.

Yves: Right.

The telephone rings.

Rachel: Check the call display.

Matt: It's Hank.

Matt answers the phone.

Rachel: And I think those brushes are dry now. They need to be sorted.

Yves: Oui.

Matt: Hey Hank.

Rachel: Hank's our lawyer slash agent slash manager.

Matt: Fox?

Rachel: We tried taking care of it ourselves at first. There's just too much to think about.

Yves: And how is the second book selling?

Rachel: Through the roof. Looks like BitchTits the Juice Pig is gonna get his own limited series.

Yves: Excellent.

Rachel: Now we just have to find time to plot it.

Yves: A BitchTits miniseries?

Matt: How much?

Rachel: It's got to be something wild. Something that makes the character sympathetic but still allows him to maintain his anti-hero status.

Yves: Oui.

Rachel: Really push the envelope. Impossible action sequences. Zany sexual situations. But with integrity.

Yves: Like what?

Rachel: I don't know. That's Matt's department.

Yves: Sounds great. When do we start?

Matt: Okay. Right. Bye.

Matt hangs up the phone.

Matt: Yes!!

Rachel: What?

Matt: There's been an offer to develop a new, animated series for Fox!

Yves: Wow.

Rachel: When do we start?

Short pause.

Matt: The offer wasn't for both of us.

Rachel: What?

Matt: They only want me.

Short pause.

Rachel: Really.

A restaurant. Martin is there. Matt joins him.

Martin: You're quiet.

Matt: Sorry. Minor crisis.

Martin: Anything you want to talk about?

Matt: Work related. There's no point discussing it until I've had some time to think about it.

Martin: Serious?

Matt: Nothing I can't handle. Being with you makes it seem less urgent now.

Martin: I think my family would like you. They don't usually approve of my taste in boys.

Matt: Have you told them about your HIV thing?

Martin: They're all older than me. I don't think they'd understand.

Matt: You should have their support.

Martin: My father still believes homosexuality is a mental disorder.

Matt: So how many people do know you're positive?

Martin: Only the ones that need to.

Matt: Sure.

Martin: It's not a secret, but it's not common knowledge.

Matt: I get it. Martin, you never got to do that wild gay kid thing. The clubs. The drugs. The other kids.

Martin: I've done my best to catch up.

Matt: I just caught the tail end of all that.

Martin reaches across the table and takes Matt's hand.

Martin: You know Matt, I haven't felt like this with anyone since I first met Yves.

Pause.

Martin: It's strange for me to be involved with someone who has their own life and agenda.

Matt: Strange good or strange bad.

Martin: Strange strange.

Matt: Can you deal with it?

Pause.

Martin: I spent the afternoon with my friend Robert. I told you about him. He's the guy who's going blind from CMV— whose neuropathy is so bad he can't walk anymore—his entire body's covered with KS lesions. The cocktail was way too late for his damaged immune system. He looks like a guy from one of those old concentration camp clips. A long time ago I promised him that if he got so sick he didn't want to go on I'd help him however I could. He decided today was the day. We only had a couple of hours before the nurse arrived. He took an overdose of morphine. It should have killed him within an hour. I promised I'd stay with him until he was gone. But it took a lot longer than we thought. He went into this sort of coma but he was making the most horrible sounds. Like a cough and snore mixed together. I kept waiting and waiting but he wouldn't die. The nurse was going to be there in fifteen minutes. I knew I had to get out before something screwed up and they revived him. So I took the pillow and held it over his face until he stopped breathing.

Matt: What kinda world do we live in?

Long pause.

Martin: Dessert?

Matt: No. *Pause. Matt takes Martin's hand.* Thank you.

Martin puts his hand over Matt's. Fade to black.

Stephanie Wolfe as Rachel and Peter Wilds as Matt. Theatre Network, Edmonton.

Bradley Moss as Yves, Robert Ouellette as Martin, and Peter Wilds as Matt. Theatre Network, Edmonton.

Bradley Moss as Yves, Robert Ouellette as Martin, and Chris Fassbender as Rex. Theatre Network, Edmonton.

ROBERT SHANNON

ROBERT SHANNON

Stephanie Wolfe as Rachel and Peter Wilds as Matt. Theatre Network, Edmonton.

Act Two

The condo. Rex is eating cereal. Martin enters dressed for work, carrying his laptop.

Martin: Did you piss the bed last night?

Rex: What?

Martin gets himself a coffee.

Martin: Your end of the hall smells like a watersports festival this morning.

Rex: I don't think so.

Martin: I know when you lose control of your bladder Rex.

Rex: I didn't piss the bed.

Martin: When you're coked and you've been drinking.

Rex finishes his cereal and stands.

Rex: I gotta get to work.

Martin: Where's Matt's pot?

Rex: What?

Martin: You told him you'd get it.

Rex: The guy took the money and split. I never saw him again.

Martin: Right.

Rex: I gotta get to work.

Martin: Look, I think it might be time we talked about re-evaluating our situation.

Rex: I have to go.

Martin: I think things are changing.

Matt: It's only an offer.

Rex: No they're not.

Rex exits, leaving his cereal bowl and box on the table. The studio. Matt and Rachel are sharing a joint.

Rachel: You want to accept it.

Rex: Bye.

Matt: I might.

Rachel: What do we do with SpumBoy and Fridge Magnet Girl?

Matt: I could do both?

Rachel: Doubt it.

Matt: I've got a while to think about it.

Rachel: Sure.

Pause.

Rachel: It's because I'm a woman.

Matt: What?

Rachel: That's why they want you and not me.

Matt: Rachel, you're an inker. No one has any idea of your gender from looking at your work.

Rachel: They see my name, they realize I'm a woman, they assume I'm the unnecessary partner.

Matt: Or it's just pencillers they're looking for.

Rachel: You're a man Matt. You don't understand how this works.

Martin: It is a problem.

Matt: How could I?

Martin: You and Rachel have worked together for a long time.

Matt: Don't sweat it Rachel. I've got some time.

Martin: She must be feeling rather inadequate.

Sound of the streetcar outside Martin's place. Matt joins Martin in the condo.

Matt: And what's fucked up in your life?

Martin: I'm having a problem with Rex.

Matt: I hate being ripped off on drug deals. What are you gonna do? Call the cops?

Martin: I'm sure he'll find a way to get it back to you.

Pause.

Matt: It appears we've reached the point in this relationship where I say what's wrong you've been very quiet lately and assume it's all because of me.

Martin: You really believe everything in the world has something to do with you, don't you?

Matt: Yes. Don't you?

Martin: Yes. It's not you Matt. Next year's an election year. I'm trying to decide if I should run again.

Matt:	Why wouldn't you?
Martin:	I've been around politics since I was twenty-two. I have to start thinking about what I want to do with the rest of my life.
Matt:	Doesn't that ever stop?
Martin:	After my HIV diagnosis I just assumed this would be my last term. I was going to retire. I was looking forward to it. Go on disability like everyone else and go to the gym every day. That's not such an option anymore.
Matt:	But you really make a difference Martin. You work harder than anyone except me. And you have to talk to people and deal with pissed off sandwich board people and go to city meetings and—everything.
Martin:	*Laughs.* You're very good for my ego Matt.
Matt:	That's why I'm here.
Martin:	Do you think Rachel's upset about the offer?
Matt:	Sure. The Fox people don't understand. Rachel makes very important contributions to the book. I think this was inevitable though.

Rachel speaks from the darkness.

Rachel:	Matt, that's great.
Matt:	It had to happen eventually.
Martin:	You're the writer.
Rachel:	You deserve it.
Martin:	You want the animation deal.
Matt:	Yeah. But I gotta respect my partner. No matter how much I want that money.
Martin:	Would Rachel find work without you?
Matt:	Sure.
Martin:	Inking for someone else?

Short pause.

Matt:	Yeah.
Martin:	You should be careful about losing people you care for Matt. Sometimes you can't find them again.
Matt:	That wouldn't happen with Rachel.
Martin:	Make sure you consider all your options.

Sound of a streetcar passing.

Matt:	You've got a hair on your back.

Martin: Yuck. Pull it out.

Matt: Sure.

Martin: Ow. Any other surprises back there?

Matt: Like a lesion?

Short pause.

Martin: Sometimes my back breaks out.

Matt: Sorry.

Martin: Natural mistake.

Matt: Sometimes I say shit without thinking.

Martin: We all do Matt. Don't worry about it.

Matt runs his fingers over Martin's back softly.

Matt: I know I shouldn't be seduced by the money but I can't help it. Money's the only real power. If you want the power to change things you have to have money. Money, intelligence, money, good looks, money, a good body, money, the right connections, money, a lot of ambition, money. Contemporary life is very demanding.

Short pause.

Martin: What did you just write on my back?

Matt: What?

Martin: You just wrote something on my back with your finger.

Matt: No. I was just touching it.

Martin: I swear you wrote something.

Matt: No.

The telephone rings.

Martin: Who'd that be at this time?

The telephone rings again. Martin answers it.

Martin: Hello?

Martin listens for a moment.

Martin: Where is he now? Okay. I'll be right there.

Matt: What's wrong?

Martin: Rex's been busted.

Matt: For dealing?

Martin: For performing lewd and indecent acts on-stage and being found in a common bawdyhouse.

Matt: Yowza!

Martin: They busted Remingtons.

Matt: It's Monday night.

Martin: Spermarama.

Matt: He wasn't.

Martin: He was.

Martin grabs Matt's coat, hands it to him, and pulls on his own jacket.

Matt: In front of everyone?

Martin: He was just finishing when the cops showed up.

Matt: Kewl.

Martin: This is just what I need.

Matt: I'll come with you.

Martin: No. Thanks.

Matt: You sure?

Martin: I'll drop you off on my way.

Matt: I can provide moral support.

Martin: I don't need any moral support.

Yves enters wearing nothing but a dingy pair of oversized jockey shorts.

Yves: I need twenty dollars to pay a taxi.

Matt: You took a cab like that?

Martin: Jesus! What happened?

Yves: Someone gave me a Valium they had left over since 1987,
I had a few cocktails, went to the Barracks, undressed,
blacked out, came to and some cunt had stolen everything.
The man working the door was kind enough to lend me
his underwear and there is a big smelly cab driver out
front with his meter running. I need the money now.

Martin: Put my robe on. Did anyone see you?

Martin hands Yves money. Yves puts on the robe.

Yves: I don't know.

Yves exits.

Martin: This shit is going to fuck me up really bad one day.

Matt: It is a bit like a Fellini movie.

Martin: Fuck.

Matt: I can't believe they busted Remingtons.

Martin: Come on.

Matt: Martin, I really think I should come.

Martin: It would only complicate things.

Matt: But if we're boyfriends then we should share—

Martin: *Cutting him off.* This is not something I want to share with you or anyone else. I'll take care of it. I told you that.

Pause.

Matt: Right.

Martin: It's between Rex and me.

Matt: Sure.

Pause.

Martin: Come on.

Rachel appears in the studio.

Rachel: So you got dumped at home?

Matt: It seems to me our police force would be serving us all better if they were out catching muggers and rapists instead of hassling a strip club.

Sound of the jackhammer. Matt and Rachel work.

Rachel: It seems like every time the world gets closer to accepting you guys something stupid like this happens and the general public ends up thinking gays are a bunch of sex-obsessed perverts.

Matt: Rachel, anything we're doing, there are more straight people out there doing the exact same thing. We're just up front about it. We may be a bunch of sex-obsessed perverts but we still have rights.

Rachel: Wanking in public?

Matt: Everyone's an adult. No one's being hurt.

Rachel: It's disgusting.

Matt: Some people think pot smokers are disgusting. Does that mean we should stop smoking weed too?

Rachel: That's different.

Matt: How?

Rachel: There's no sex involved.

Matt: You're smoking dope with the wrong people hon.

Yves enters.

Matt: Salut.

Yves: Sorry I am late. I had to stop at the doctor's office on my way.

Rachel: No problem. Everything work out last night?

Yves: Yes.

Matt: I've got all the original pages on the work table. I'd like you to go through them and arrange them chronologically. Check with me if there's any missing. We've sold some.

Yves: I thought we might talk about the BitchTits miniseries this morning—

Matt: Actually Yves, we're running a little late on this issue. We're gonna back-burner that mini for a bit—

Sound of the jackhammer.

Matt: I am going to go out there and shoot those people.

Yves: Issue one. Page five?

Matt: Sold it. Did you see Martin today?

Yves: Oui. He had to take the morning off to deal with Rex.

Matt: Someone's in deep shit.

Yves: Do not be so sure.

Matt: Why?

Yves: Rex has Martin wrapped around his finger. He always has.

Matt: Well Martin sounds like he's getting fed up with the whole deal.

Yves: Martin—he loves to come to the rescue. Issue four page six?

Pause.

Yves: Matt?

Matt: What?

Yves: Issue four page six?

Rachel: Sold it. You okay?

Matt: Fine.

Yves stops shuffling through the pages.

Yves: Of course now that Martin has met you, Rex might find things have changed.

Martin: What the hell were you thinking?

Yves: Maybe not.

Martin and Rex at Martin's place.

Rex: I needed the money.

Martin: A hundred and fifty bucks?

Rex: It's two hundred if you come.

Martin: What about your job?

Rex: I lost my job weeks ago.

Martin: Rex, I've thought long and hard about this and I really think it's time you got your own place.

Rex: You know I don't have any money to get my own place.

Martin: Whose fault is that?

Rex: Jesus Martin, don't start.

Martin: You knew the rules when you came back here. No coke. No trouble.

Rex: I have no place to go. I have no money. Please don't throw me out.

Martin: I spoke to George this morning. As the owner of the bar he's going to cover all the legal costs.

Rex: Don't throw me out.

Martin: We can't keep doing this.

Rex: Please.

Pause.

Martin: You look tired.

Rex: I didn't get much sleep last night.

Martin moves behind Rex and massages his shoulders.

Martin: Relax. Your shoulders are so tense.

Rex: What do you expect?

Martin: Let's work those knots out of there.

Rex: You're the only one who's ever looked after me.

Martin: Yeah.

Rex: It usta be real fun.

Martin: Yes.

Martin's hands stray down to Rex's chest. He strokes Rex's nipples. After a moment Rex stands and takes Martin's hand seductively.

Rex: I think I'm gonna go to bed now.

Martin: Yes.

Rex: You wanna be my dad?

Long pause. Martin takes his hand from Rex reluctantly.

Martin: I have to get to the office.

Matt: The Deceptive Elf.

Rex: Just give me a little time to get on my feet.

Matt: Separatist spy.

Martin: No more coke. No more trouble.

Rachel: Why do the French want to separate?

The studio. Matt and Rachel are drawing. Yves is sorting through invoices.

Rex: No more coke. No more trouble.

Yves: We have never gotten along with the English.

Rex: Promise.

Matt: I'm pretty dodgy on that part of our history.

Yves: My Papa used to say that English Canada was made on the backs of the French.

Rachel: My father usta say Central Canada was supported by the sweat of the Maritimers.

Matt: Everyone in Calgary thinks the East's supported by the work of the Prairie Provinces.

Rachel: And B.C.'s so far away we don't care what they think.

Matt: People from Saskatchewan are very nice.

Rachel: They have to be. They're from Saskatchewan.

Yves: Quebec is a distinct society.

Matt: This entire country is composed of distinct societies. Yves I need a couple more sheets of bristol board. The two ply.

Yves: Oui.

Yves gets the bristol for Matt.

Matt: I love Quebec. Montreal's my favorite city.

Yves: Montréal is not all Québèc.

Rachel: There's more?

Matt: Quebec's the only thing that makes Canada interesting.

Rachel: Don't forget Anne of Green Gables.

Matt: Quebec and Anne of Green Gables.

Yves: The French feel the same way. And they resent it.

Matt: Why would we break up this amazing landmass over a language issue? There must be some compromise.

Yves: If you have not been a minority lost in the majority you cannot understand.

Matt: Well actually...

Rachel: *Cuts them off.* Guys, politics don't pay the rent.

Yves: I thought you might show me how it is you put all this together today.

Matt: Not today man. I'm meeting Martin in a coupla hours. I'm going to watch a council meeting today.

Pause.

Yves: Good luck to stay awake.

Rachel: That bad?

Yves: Oui.

Matt joins Martin at a restaurant table.

Martin: You still haven't said anything about the council meeting.

Gradual fade in of restaurant noises.

Matt: Some of those civic politicians really need to go out and do some ecstasy and get fucked up the ass.

Martin: Are you saying that's what makes me good?

Matt: It helps.

Martin: How's Yves working out?

Matt: He wants to be a full-time creative partner before he's been an assistant.

Martin: You'll find that about Yves.

Matt: Yeah?

Martin: His ambition often overreaches his grasp.

Matt: He doesn't seem to have a lot of patience.

Martin: He never did. I don't know what he'd do without me.

Matt: And Rex?

Martin: Still looking for a job.

Matt: Martin, what do you get out of your relationships with these guys?

Martin: Well Yves gives me energy and Rex—he needs someone to look out for him.

Matt: Has it ever occurred to you that maybe you're not helping them out so much by taking care of everything for them.

Martin: What would either of them have done without me there?

Matt: Learned their lessons and quit doing stupid shit.

Martin: They're bad boys. What can I say?

Matt: After a certain age you stop being a bad boy and become a loser.

Pause.

Martin: It's really none of your business Matt.

Matt: Okay.

Pause.

Martin: I'm just a bit tired.

Matt: Look, I thought—if your schedule could handle it—we might think about taking a quick weekend trip to New York.

Martin: I couldn't afford that right now.

Matt: I don't mind picking up the tab.

Martin: I wouldn't feel right letting you pay.

Matt: You let me pay for everything else.

Martin: I don't know if I want to take a weekend trip with you Matt.

Pause.

Matt: Ah.

Martin: I feel like I'm getting into something I have no control over.

Matt: I thought that's how relationships worked.

Martin: I think we have to stop spending so much time together.

Matt: Did I do something wrong?

Martin: Matt, I'm just asking for a little room. You're a bit—intense.

Matt: *Intensely.* I'm not intense.

Martin: Being with you demands a lot of energy.

Matt: I feel like you're dumping me.

Martin: I'm not dumping you.

Matt: What are you doing then?

Pause.

Martin: I've decided not to run for election next year.

Matt: Really?

Martin: I need some time to think about where I'm going.

Matt: Good.

Pause.

Matt: I stopped taking my Prozac.

Martin: Why?

Matt: Now that I've found that middle place I'm not sure I like being there all the time. I think I'd rather visit when I need to.

Martin: I see.

Matt: And because I wanted to come with you. Tonight.

Pause.

Martin: I'm not really up for it tonight. We'll take a rain check.

Matt: Good night.

Rachel working in the studio. It's very late.

Rachel: Prozac? You never told me you were taking Prozac.

Matt: I didn't want to worry you.

Rachel: I should know if you're depressed.

Matt: I'm not depressed. I'm just not—good enough.

Rachel: The two of you have been pretty intense.

Matt: It's the HIV thing. When he told me and I decided I'd still go for it I think I made some kind of commitment inside myself. I just assumed he made the same commitment.

Rachel: Don't make it an issue till it's an issue Matt. I'm gonna head. I've got plans. You need a ride?

Matt: No thanks. I feel like walking.

Martin working in the condo. Rex enters.

Rex: Hey.

Rachel: 'night.

Martin: Hey, I was hoping you'd get home before I turned in.

Rex: Yeah.

Short pause.

Martin: You're stoned.

Rex: I need some money.

Martin: I have no more money.

Rex: I need some money now Martin. I owe Edgar some money — a lot of money—and if he doesn't get some money tonight this boy's in deep shit.

Martin: There's no money left Rex. I'm broke.

Rex: A coupla hundred bucks'd keep him happy.

Martin: You're just going to spend it on coke.

Rex: Look asshole, you're the reason I'm hooked on this shit!

Martin: Don't start that again.

Rex: I never did coke before I met you. I wouldn't be here if you didn't tell me how much I'd like it just so you could get me to bend over that first time.

Martin: It was your idea.

Rex: It was the only way I could go to bed with you.

Martin: Shut up Rex!

Rex: And now I'm fucked up and it's your fault!

Martin: I've tried to make it up to you.

Rex: By using my ass whenever the tab got too high.

Martin: You loved that deal.

Rex: You told me you'd take care of me.

Martin: You said you'd never leave me.

Rex: I said anything for drugs.

Martin: You really have overstayed your welcome Rex.

Rex: I'm staying as long as I want to Martin.

Martin: No.

Rex: You owe me and I'm gonna collect.

Martin: I got infected after you stopped sleeping with me.

Rex: That's my fault?

Martin: I wouldn't've been out there getting my brains fucked out if you hadn't broken it off with me.

Rex: You are so fulla shit—

Martin suddenly grabs Rex by the shirt and shakes him violently.

Martin: You should have this fucking thing too!

Pause. Rex pulls away from Martin carefully.

Rex: You'd like that, wouldn't you?

Pause.

Martin: No. I'm sorry.

Pause.

Martin: We're even Rex. We're both fucked up. Okay? Good-bye.

Rex: Gonna take my keys from me?

Rex holds the keys out to Martin.

Martin: I'll change the locks—

Rex: I'll break a window. I'll wake the neighbours up and tell them I've lost my keys. I'll go to the press and tell them—

Martin: Stop it Rex!

Rex: Take my keys.

Pause. Martin does nothing.

Rex: How much money do you have on you?

Martin: About sixty bucks.

Rex: Give it to me.

Martin shoves the money into Rex's hand.

Rex: Thanks. I'll be back later. And stay out of my room. My ass belongs to me now.

Rex exits. Long pause. Martin is very angry. He is having trouble keeping himself under control.

Lights rise on the studio. Matt and Rachel are working. Day.

Matt: Where the hell's Yves?

Rachel: This is the second time he's been late this week.

Matt: I'm sure he'll give us the doctor excuse again.

Rachel: He sure spends a lot of time at the doctor's.

Matt: Having AIDS will do that to you.

Rachel: You didn't tell me he had AIDS.

Matt: I didn't think it was important.

Rachel: Seems to be a lot you're not telling me.

Matt: Rachel, I spend ten to twelve hours a day with you. I can't tell you everything.

Rachel: I just want to know the important stuff.

Pause.

Rachel: Cam called for you last night. I forgot to tell you.

Matt: Did he leave a message?

Rachel: He's out of the hospital and bored. Wants you to call him.

Matt: Tomorrow. For sure. What'd you do last night?

Rachel: Went for drinks with The Girls. Half of us moaned about the men we don't have in our lives, the other half moaned about the men they do have in their lives. It's like nobody's connecting.

Matt: Maybe condoms are the problem.

Rachel: Condoms?

Matt: There's something about being inside someone, uncovered, unprotected, that connects people.

Rachel: Thought about the Fox thing?

Matt: Yeah.

Rachel: And?

Matt: You're my partner. Whatever we decide has to be decided together.

Rachel: But you want to do it.

Matt: I want to consider it very carefully.

Rachel: Should I remind you we started doing SpumBoy and Fridge Magnet Girl because we were fed up with gutless mainstream entertainment.

Matt: I know. But things have changed. We're in our thirties Rachel. It's time to sell out.

Rachel: Who are you? What have you done with Matt?

Matt: Come on—

Rachel: You've been spending too much time with politicians.

Yves enters.

Matt: We need you here when you say you're going to be here.

Yves: So I can sweep up and arrange files?

Matt: Yes.

Yves: That is not what I was hired to do.

Matt: That's exactly what you were hired to do.

Yves: You said I would get to draw.

Matt: You know, if you're going to be resentful we can find another assistant.

Yves: I am grateful for the work.

Rachel: Everything okay Yves?

Short pause.

Yves: Sure.

Matt hands a number of finished pages to Yves and a single page to Rachel.

Matt: Those pages need to have the graphite erased. Careful around the fine lines.

Yves: Oui.

Rachel: What is this?

Matt: What?

Rachel: This background imagery behind SpumBoy's story about killing his dying friend?

Matt: The camps.

Rachel: The Nazi death camps?

Matt: Yeah.

Rachel: You can't do this Matt.

Matt: What?

Rachel: You can't use this as background imagery for something that's about gays dying of AIDS.

Matt: Why not?

Rachel: It's offensive.

Matt: Offensive?!

Rachel: Millions of Jews died.

Matt: Thousand of gays died. And the ones who survived weren't freed with everyone else after the liberation. They were thrown in prison again for being gay.

Rachel: People will be pissed off.

Matt: That isn't always a bad thing.

Rachel: You know I'm Jewish.

Matt: Oh please.

Yves: You are Jewish?

Rachel: Yeah.

Matt: She's about as Jewish as I am Christian.

Yves: You do not look Jewish.

Rachel: My parents didn't tell me until I was sixteen. My grandparents were in the camps and never got over it. It did something really fucked up to my parents. It took me a long time to figure out they didn't hate religion, they hated God. For letting it happen I guess. They never talked about the past. But it still doesn't excuse what was done to my grandparents.

Matt: Or anyone. That's my point.

Rachel: It's exploitive.

Matt: It is not exploitive.

Rachel: You're just using easy imagery to shock people.

Matt: Rachel, would you feel this way if it was someone from another group telling the story? Someone who wasn't queer?

Rachel: I don't want to ink it.

Rachel sets the page back on Matt's drawing board.

Matt: Then maybe you shouldn't be working with me.

Rachel: Maybe I shouldn't. It provides you with a perfect excuse to sell out and go to Hollywood.

Matt: It's called growing Rachel.

Rachel: Growing?

Matt: Finding new challenges. Moving forward. Something that seems to terrify you.

Rachel: You're the one that hogs the limelight.

Matt: You get all the same opportunities I do.

Rachel: No I don't.

Matt: Well maybe if you had more of a sense of humour and less of a social conscience you would.

Rachel: And maybe if you stopped singing and dancing for five minutes and let someone else show off once in a while Fox would be calling me too.

Matt: Don't count on it.

Rachel: Fuck you.

Pause.

Matt: This is an issue.

Rachel: This is an issue.

The telephone rings. Matt answers the phone.

Matt: Hey. Really? Okay. I'll be right down.

Matt hangs up.

Matt: Martin's downstairs. Something's wrong. I have to go.

Pause.

Matt: Yves, do you have any idea what this is all about?

Yves: It is not my place to say.

Matt exits.

Yves: Things sure get weird fast.

Rachel: Sure do.

Pause.

Rachel: Fuck.

Canada's Wonderland. Day. Matt and Martin are at the roller coaster.

Matt: Martin say something.

Martin: Just relax Matt.

Matt: But this is so weird. There's hardly anyone here. What's going on?

Martin: I want to ride the roller coaster.

Matt: You know I hate these things.

Martin: Please.

They get onto the roller coaster. The announcer is heard. It starts.

Matt: What's this about?

Martin: Take my hand.

Matt takes Martin's hand. Pause.

Martin: There's been some trouble Matt.

Matt: What kind of trouble?

Martin: With Rex.

Matt: I don't like it when you do this Martin.

Martin: Possible legal trouble.

Matt: It's always something that really fucks me up.

Martin: Rex is threatening to lay sexual assault charges against me.

The roller coaster stops suddenly, suspended in time and space. Matt stares at Martin in disbelief.

Matt: Sexual assault?

Martin: He was stoned again. Wanted money. We had a fight. I tried to throw him out but he wouldn't give me his keys. He told me if I threw him out he'd go to the press.

Matt: And tell them what?

Martin: That I was a cokehead—that I'm HIV positive. Anything. I didn't know what to do. He went out. I tried to go to sleep but I couldn't. I was so upset Matt.

Matt: What did you do?

Martin: He came back later. Really stoned. I heard him stumble into his room and close the door. I know how he gets when he's like that—dead the second he hits the bed.

Matt: And?

Martin: I went into his room, pulled the covers back, turned him over, pulled his shorts down and greased up his asshole.

Matt: Jesus.

Martin: Then I left the room.

The roller coaster starts again, faster this time.

Matt: That is seriously fucked up.

Martin: I had to get rid of him.

Matt: Was there a condom in the scenario?

Martin: No.

Matt: Why didn't you call the cops or have someone help you get rid of his stuff or—

Martin: I just had to get him out.

The roller coaster stops. Matt and Martin disembark.

Matt: Martin, he's going to have people thinking you raped him and infected him. He could go to the cops.

Martin: He just wants money.

Matt: It's going to get out. At least let people know he's an extortionist. It'll make you look better.

Martin: I can take a second mortgage on the condo. Rex knows this is a one-time-only deal but he's promised to keep his mouth shut if I come up with the money. He says he'll leave town.

Matt: Martin, he threatened to go to the press and you decided to deal with it by sticking your finger up his ass and making him think you raped him?

Martin: It was a mistake.

Matt: Didn't you think of that?

Martin: I just wanted to—hurt him.

Matt: Is he that important?

Martin: If I'd wanted to I could have done the real thing. Easily.

Matt: But you didn't?

Martin: Jesus Matt. No!

Pause.

Martin: I wanted to. But I didn't.

Pause.

Matt: I have to go.

Martin: I'm pretty desperate for a friend right now.

Matt: I just need a little time.

Martin: Matt.

Matt: Yeah.

Martin: I didn't rape him.

Yves: Bullshit.

Matt: I know.

The studio. Yves is cutting bristol into drawing sheets with a paper cutter. Rachel is inking.

Yves: Any idiot could do what I am doing.

Matt: Please take me home.

Rachel: Y'know Yves, we're both beginning to have a bit of a problem with your attitude.

Yves: Is that so?

Rachel: You can't just walk in and expect to start at the top. It doesn't work that way.

Yves: Oui.

Yves cuts another piece of paper.

Yves: I don't expect Matt will be back right away.

Rachel: Why not?

Yves: He might be a little—uh—upset.

Rachel: Why?

Yves: Matt sees Martin with eyes like a girl. He does not see the true Martin.

Rachel: And I suppose you do.

Yves: I know him very well. Martin tries very hard to be someone he is not—tries not to do things he likes to do. But Martin is not always so strong. Martin likes control and he will never have control with Matt.

Rachel: True.

Yves cuts another piece of paper.

Yves: Martin raped Rex last night.

Rachel: What?

Yves: While Rex was passed out. Without a condom.

Rachel: Who told you this?

Yves: Rex.

Rachel: What I've heard about Rex doesn't make him the most reliable person in my book.

Yves: Oui. But he is not lying about this.

Rachel: How do you know?

Yves: I know.

Yves stacks the paper he has cut.

Yves: Matt does not know Martin.

Rachel: No?

Yves: Martin does not know Martin.

Rachel: I suppose you do?

Yves: Y'a personne qui connaît personne. *(No one knows anyone.)*

Rachel: What?

Yves: Martin and Rex have had a daddy game from the beginning of their relationship. Rex cannot admit he likes to get fucked so Martin does it to him while Rex is sleeping. Rex cries no no but that is part of the game.

Rachel: This's been going on while Matt's been seeing Martin?

Yves: It is how Rex pays the rent. I was with Rex all morning. He is going to press charges against Martin.

Rachel: Why are you telling me this?

Yves: I do not want Matt to be hurt.

Rachel: If you didn't want Matt to be hurt you would've kept your mouth shut.

Yves: You do not have to tell him.

Rachel: What are you getting from this Yves?

Yves: When I was twenty-five Martin broke up with me for an eighteen-year-old neither of us remembers anymore. I went mad. Did stupid shit. Let guys fuck me bare when I was high. I was infected. The boy left Martin a few months later. Martin came crawling to me to take him back. He said it was all a mistake. He promised to take care of me. Always.

Rachel: Why did he get involved with Matt then?

Yves: Martin wants to see if he is strong enough to change the way he is.

Rachel: Fuck.

Yves: Do not feel sorry for Matt. Matt has everything.

Pause.

Yves: There is a rumour in the community that Martin fucks boys without a condom whenever they will let him. Even though they know he is positive. Many do it.

Rachel: And you don't call him on it?

Yves: *Shrugs.* He pays the bills.

Rachel: It doesn't bother you being a parasite?

Yves: No more than it bothers you.

Rachel: Fuck you.

Yves: You mean, if you did not have Matt, your inking is so good you would be successful without him?

Rachel: I don't know.

Yves: Perhaps you will find out when he takes the Fox deal.

Rachel: Maybe.

Yves: And then you can ink only those things that reflect your opinion of the world.

Rachel: Don't even try that with me.

Yves: Perhaps you will find someone straight to work with.

Rachel: You'd better leave now.

Yves: That's what you really want, isn't it? Someone more like you. Someone a lot like Matt. Only straight.

Rachel: Good-bye Yves.

Pause.

Yves: Bonsoir homophobe.

Rachel: You're wrong on that one asshole.

Yves: Am I?

Yves exits. Rachel sits at her drawing board for a moment then takes the page from Matt's drawing board and slowly begins to ink it. Matt enters and moves to his drawing board without looking at Rachel. He begins to work. Neither says anything for a long moment. Rachel speaks quietly and carefully.

Rachel: Rex told Yves everything this morning. About the rape.

Matt: Rape?

Rachel: Isn't that what Martin told you?

Matt: Martin told me he set Rex up to think he'd been raped.

Rachel: Did Martin tell you he got to cornhole Rex for the rent?

Matt: He used to—

Rachel: Yves says it's been going on the whole time.

Matt: Yves doesn't know shit.

Rachel: Have you heard the rumour about Martin fucking guys without a condom?

Matt: I don't listen to rumours.

Rachel: Matt, this whole thing stinks.

Matt: It is complicated.

Rachel: Matt, it's a fucking horror show! Rape. HIV infection. This isn't normal behaviour.

Matt: It is in my world.

Rachel: Then there's something wrong with your world.

Matt: Don't start on how fucked up my world is Rachel.

Rachel: It's sick.

Matt: Well what do you expect when you live a world where most people tell you you're sick. A world where everyone's already sick or scared of getting sick or trying to make other people sick. Sometimes I wonder if it's possible for any of us to be healthy.

Rachel: You can't ignore this Matt.

Matt: Do you think Martin's a rapist?

Pause.

Rachel: I've never trusted him.

Matt: I thought you liked him.

Rachel: I do. But he's a politician Matt. They make their living by telling people what they want to hear.

Pause.

Matt: I feel like the heroine in one of those Alfred Hitchcock movies where everyone knows more than she does.

Rachel: When the term pressing charges enters a relationship it's time for some serious examination.

Matt turns, Martin is seen in the condo. Matt joins him immediately.

Matt: Why is Yves telling people you raped Rex?

Rachel: No matter how hard it is.

Martin: What?

Matt: That's what he told Rachel.

Sound of a streetcar passing.

Martin: He's probably just upset.

Matt: So he won't tell anyone except the person most likely to tell me?

Martin: I—he told Rachel?

Matt: Doesn't Yves know what really happened?

Martin: Of course.

Matt: Then why'd he tell that to Rachel?

Martin: I've never done anything to Rex against his will—ever.

Matt: Just sneaked into his room at night so you could play your repressed little daddy game.

Martin: None of that went on while I was seeing you.

Matt: That's not what I was told.

Martin: It's the truth.

Matt: Yeah?

Martin: You and I live in different worlds Matt.

Matt: You think just because I'm not infected with HIV I'm not living with it as well.

Martin: You don't have the disease.

Matt: Sometimes I wish I did. At least that way I'd have an excuse to give up and be irresponsible too.

Martin: That's unfair.

Matt: Martin, you were forty-three years old when you tested positive. Forty-three.

Martin: I'm supposed to be perfect because I'm over forty?

Matt:	People look up to you.
Martin:	I'm not responsible for other people's actions.
Matt:	You're supposed to be a leader.
Martin:	Have you been carrying this resentment around ever since I told you?
Matt:	I guess I have.
Martin:	I knew it.
Matt:	How are we supposed to fight all the other battles we need to fight when this fucking disease keeps sucking up all of our energy?
Martin:	I don't know.
Matt:	I looked up to you Martin. From the first time I ever saw you on that boring city hall channel I thought there's a guy who has it together, who's managed to sidestep all the self-hatred I see in this community every day. We talked about being role models for Christ's sake.
Martin:	It was a mistake.
Matt:	Everything's a mistake with you Martin. You don't come out until you're thirty-five. It's a mistake. You get infected with HIV. It's a mistake. You stick something up Rex's ass. It's a mistake. Can you not see a pattern here?
Martin:	Everyone makes mistakes.
Matt:	Not those mistakes. Not everyone.
Martin:	You're mad at me for not being perfect.
Matt:	Oh please—
Martin:	You thought I'd have the answers didn't you? You thought, because I was older than you, it would be easier, didn't you?
Matt:	Yeah. I did.
Martin:	I'm human Matt.
Matt:	It's fucked Martin. The whole situation.
Martin:	I've dealt with Rex.
Matt:	And will you pay Yves off so he stops telling people you're a rapist?
Martin:	Yves needs me.
Matt:	Yves would be fine without you. He'd probably actually accomplish something if you cut him loose.
Martin:	You have no right to judge my life.
Matt:	You brought me into it.

Martin: Only because you wanted it so much.

Matt: Okay! I desperately wanted to be part of your life. You seemed to like me. Why is that a problem?

Martin: It's—everything's changed. Things just get out of control. They've been out of control ever since...

Matt: You were infected?

Martin: Since I turned forty.

Matt: So this is what I have to look forward to in middle age? Being just as fucked up only better at hiding it. Great.

Martin: It's like none of the rules make any sense.

Matt: I thought I understood you Martin.

Martin: There's no understanding it Matt.

Matt: I don't understand convincing boys to let you fuck them without a rubber.

Martin: Don't believe everything you hear.

Matt: Is that a denial Councillor?

Martin: I've never done anything with anyone that wasn't consensual.

Matt: Including your infection?

Pause.

Matt: I can't believe this. No matter what the truth is there's no way we can keep seeing each other.

Martin: What do you want me to say Matt? I'm a fuck-up? Okay, I'm a fuck-up. I made a mistake. A stupid mistake that's going to be with me for the rest of my life. I've made a whole lot of mistakes. I'll probably make a lot more. I failed and you succeeded. I'm positive. You're not. I'm weak. You're not. You can't be mad at me for not being who you wanted me to be.

Matt: I'm mad at you for not being who you represent yourself to be.

Martin: Things can change.

Pause.

Matt: Give them up.

Martin: Rex is gone.

Matt: And Yves.

Pause.

Martin: I can't.

Matt: Why not?

Martin: I promised him I'd take care of him.

Matt: I can't have a relationship with the two of you.

Martin: I can't break this promise Matt.

Matt: No. I wouldn't want you to.

Pause.

Matt: I really really liked you.

Martin starts to move toward him.

Martin: Matt—

Matt stops Martin with an upraised hand.

Matt: Don't. I can't.

Martin: But I don't want to—

Matt: *Cuts him off.* Me either. But there's no other choice. Sorry.

Matt exits leaving Martin alone for a moment.

Martin: Fuck. Fuck! Fuck!!

Pause. Yves enters.

Martin: Why did you tell him?

Yves: Je lui ai pas dit à lui. Je l'ai dit à son ami. *(I didn't tell him. I told his friend.)*

Martin: Was he such a threat?

Yves: Tu le niaisais. *(You were toying with him.)*

Martin: J'aimais bien Matt. *(I liked Matt.)*

Yves: Matt est pas comme nous. *(Matt is not like us.)*

Martin: No. He's not.

Matt and Rachel are seen in the studio.

Matt: Martin and I just broke up.

Rachel: You okay?

Matt: No.

Yves: Ça aurait jamais marché. *(It never would've worked.)*

Martin: No.

Yves: Why do you look at me like that?

Pause.

Yves: Martin?

Martin: Leave me alone Yves.

The light on Yves and Martin goes out.

Matt: The three-month curse strikes again.

Rachel: Shit.

Matt: You think I should take the Fox deal?

Pause.

Rachel: I think I would.

Pause.

Matt: You would too wouldn't you?

Rachel: Much as I hate to admit it, yes I would.

Matt exits the studio quickly.

Matt: I gotta go.

A quiet female voice is heard over a sound system.

Announcer: Flight 707 to Vancouver is now available for boarding. All passengers please proceed to the departure gate.

Yves and Rex are at the airport. Rex carries a knapsack containing all of his worldly possessions.

Rex: Thanks for the ride.

Yves: You will like the west coast. It is so beautiful.

Rex: I need the money now Yves.

Yves: It is all right here.

Yves hands Rex a fat envelope.

Rex: All of it?

Yves: Minus ten percent.

Rex: For what?

Yves: The ride.

Rex: You are such an asshole.

Yves: I know.

Rex: I'm so glad to be leaving this shithole.

Yves: He used to do it to me too. When I was sleeping.

Rex: Did you like it?

Yves: Yes. You?

Rex: Usually. But it got fucked up. You guys are all fucked up.

Yves: And you.

Rex: I'm twenty-three. I'm supposed to be fucked up. I don't plan to be like this when I'm thirty.

Yves: No one does.

Rex: Well you have him all to yourself now.

Yves: That is the way it will always be.

Rex: Why?

Pause.

Yves: I love Martin. I always have.

Rex: Right.

Yves: Don't worry. You will find someone else to look after you.

Rex: I think I'll look after myself from now on. Good luck.

Yves: And good luck to you Raymond.

Rex: How the hell did you find out my real name?

Yves: I have my ways. Good-bye.

Yves winks at Rex and exits. A light on Rachel working at the drawing board. Matt enters.

Rachel: You look terrible.

Matt: I've been drinking.

Rachel: For two days?

Matt: For twenty years. But the last two days have been particularly trying.

Rachel: I was worried. Yves came by yesterday for his last cheque.

Matt: Of course he did.

Rachel: He was very friendly. Acted as if everything was just fine.

Matt: I wish there was an island—a place for gay men and women to live on our own without the straight world to tell us how different we are.

Rachel: Do you really think that would make it better?

Matt: Sometimes.

Rachel: It'd be hard for us to hang out in a place like that.

Matt: We'd take cabs.

Pause.

Matt: Last night—it was the height of my tear—I was hammered, hung around the Barn until cut off and went to the St. Marc's baths, smoked a few jays in my room, thought I'd get at least sucked off, whatever. This hot guy maybe twenty-three or twenty-four walked past my room a coupla times, definitely interested. I asked him in. He closed the door and dropped his towel. He looked like a Tom of Finland drawing. We got into bed, one thing led to another until finally he got on his back and held his legs up for me. I told him I didn't have a condom. He said he didn't care.

Rachel: Oh man...

Matt: And I rode him bareback.

Pause.

Rachel: Why?

Matt: Because he was beautiful. Because I was drunk and didn't care whether I lived or died. Because nothing makes any sense and I wanted to have that kind of intimate contact with someone—anyone—just so I didn't feel so goddamn alone. Because I'm tired of always thinking about being safe. Because I'm tired of worrying about AIDS. Because maybe it would make me like Martin and everything would be okay then.

Rachel: Matt, what did he do to your head?

Matt: It's something much bigger than Martin.

Rachel: I don't understand you guys. I'm sorry. I try to. I really do. But it's like watching a *National Geographic* special about some distant tribe or something. I just can't relate. Straight men are mystifying enough. How could I hope to understand gay men?

Matt: Cocksucking hasn't gotten me very far, but it's certainly taken me places.

Rachel laughs.

Matt: What happened to the jackhammer?

Rachel: What?

Matt: The jackhammer. We haven't heard it for a week.

Rachel: Didn't even notice. Look, I know you're going to take the Fox deal. I can live with that. I want to take over pencilling SpumBoy and Fridge Magnet Girl. We'll get a second inker.

Matt: You think you can handle that?

Rachel moves to her drawing board and takes a page from it. She hands the page to Matt.

Rachel: I made a few adjustments to the Holocaust thing. I hope you don't mind?

Matt: Adjustments?

Rachel: Additions actually.

Matt examines the page.

Matt: You included Fridge Magnet Girl.

Rachel: It didn't seem right to exclude her. Or intellectuals, or gypsies or whoever else got the shit kicked out of them by the Nazis. I mean, why hog the Holocaust right?

Matt: I can hardly tell which figures are yours and which are mine.

Rachel: So we both plot it, you'll have time for that, then I pencil it and do the dialogue and we'll get some young hotshot to ink it.

Matt: If you're up for it I'll do whatever I can.

Rachel: And when we get back together again we both have a whole new set of skills to share.

Matt: You become me.

Rachel: Yeah.

Matt: And I became Martin.

Pause.

Rachel: Do you think you're infected?

Matt: I don't know. It didn't last very long. I started to think about the whole thing and lost my rod. He lost interest. I went home.

Rachel: But what if you were exposed?

Matt: I'll get tested tomorrow. And again in three months.

Rachel: You can't do shit like that Matt.

Matt: I know. I just—just couldn't help myself. It was like it was programmed into me. I couldn't stop it.

Rachel: Don't cry.

Matt: I knew it was wrong but I didn't care.

Rachel moves to Matt and puts her arms around him.

Rachel: It's alright.

Matt: It just happened. Like to someone else. I was watching but I couldn't stop it.

Rachel: It'll be okay.

Matt: I couldn't control it.

Rachel: Ssh.

Matt: It was a mistake.

Sound of a streetcar. The condo. Martin is at the window. Yves is preparing to go out.

Yves: Rex is gone for good.

Martin: I wasn't thinking about Rex.

Yves: Matt?

Martin: He never asked me for anything.

Yves: Why would he?

Lights rise on Matt and Rachel together.

Matt: It all seems so goddamn hopeless.

Rachel: You've just been shitkicked guy.

Martin: Where will you go?

Yves: Woodys. There is a show tonight.

Rachel: You've been through a bad relationship. You've been fucked around. It's happened before and it'll happen again. You will recover.

Matt: That's the last thing I want to hear right now.

Rachel: And only your partner would say it.

A light rises on Rex alone.

Martin: Have a good time.

Yves: Would you like to come?

Martin: No. Thank you.

Yves: Please.

Martin: No.

Matt: Thank you.

Yves: Very well.

Matt: It means a lot.

Yves: *Ashamed.* J'ai besoin d'argent. *(I need some money.)*

Matt: You mean a lot.

Martin: Right.

Martin hands Yves some money.

Yves: Merci.

Matt: Thank you.

The lights on the characters fade but linger for a moment longer on Matt and Martin. They look at one another sadly. Martin looks back to Yves. Matt looks back to Rachel. Fade to black.

BRAD FRASER BIO

Brad Fraser was born in Edmonton, Alberta, Canada on June 28, 1959. His family led a nomadic existence, covering much of the interior of B.C. and rural Alberta before finally settling again in Edmonton in the early Seventies. Brad won his first playwriting competition at the age of 17 and has been writing plays ever since. He wrote and directed his first produced play, *Mutants*, for Edmonton's community theatre group Walterdale Theatre for the 1980-81 season. During the seasons he worked at Walterdale Brad also acted in, designed, directed and stage-managed a number of other shows. The following season 25th Street Theatre in Saskatoon premiered *Wolfboy*, with further productions at Theatre Network, Edmonton; Touchstone Theatre, Vancouver; and Theatre Muraille, Toronto. Two other works were performed at Passe Muraille: *Rude Noises (For a Blank Generation)*, a collective creation with Paul Thompson in 1982 and *Young Art* in 1986. Fraser subsequently wrote *Chainsaw Love* (1985) and *The Return of the Bride* (1988) for the Edmonton Fringe Festival.

In 1986 Fraser became resident playwright at Edmonton's Workshop West Theatre. Here he began working on what would eventually become known as *Unidentified Human Remains and the True Nature of Love*. This show premiered in Calgary at Alberta Theatre Projects' annual PlayRites Festival in 1989. With this play Fraser achieved national and international recognition with productions across the globe. The show has been translated into many languages and continues to enjoy worldwide acclaim. The movie version, directed by Denys Arcand, was released in 1994. Fraser won a Genie award for his cinematic adaptation of the play.

For three seasons Fraser wrote and directed plays for the Edmonton Teen Festival of the Arts: *Blood Buddies* (written with Jeffrey Hirschfield, 1989); a highly revised *Young Art* (1990); and

Prom Night of the Living Dead, with music by Darrin Hagen (1991).

Fraser's *The Ugly Man* also premiered at the PlayRites Festival in 1992 with subsequent productions in Montreal, Brighton, Edmonton, London, Hamburg and other cities. The French version of *The Ugly Man* (*L'homme laid*) as well as the French version of *Remains* (*Des restes humains non identifiés et la véritable nature de l'amour*) were published by Boreal Press in 1993. Both productions, as well as a French version of *Poor Super Man* were produced at Théâtre de Quat'Sous in Montreal.

Poor Super Man opened in Cincinnati 1994 after considerable publicity and controversy. As was the case with *Remains*, the script was named by *Time* magazine as one of the top ten plays of the year and went on to further acclaim and productions world-wide. Fraser has adapted his play for the screen and is signed to direct it for Edmonton's Real Time Films in the spring of 1999.

Brad's newest play, *Snake in Fridge*, was commissioned by the Royal Exchange Theatre in Manchester, England and is set to premiere in their 1999-2000 season. Fraser is also at work at a reinvented version of the musical *Outrageous*. An adaptation of the 1978 movie of the same name, Brad is working with composer Joey Miller and the Canadian Stage Company to ready the show for its opening sometime after the year 2000.

In addition to his work for the theatre Brad Fraser has also written extensively for radio, film, television and print media. He is a regular contributor and columnist for *FAB National*, Canada's national gay magazine. Brad has been nominated for and received numerous awards for his writing, directing and acting over the course of his career. He is a five-time winner of the Alberta Culture Playwrighting competition, a two-time winner of Toronto's prestigious Chalmers Award, a recipient of the London Evening Standard Award, the L.A. Critic's Award, the Dora Mavor Moore Award and many others. *Poor Super Man* was nominated for the Governor General's Award for Drama (1995) and Brad has also won the Writers' Guild of Alberta Award for Drama for *Poor Super Man* and for *Love and Human Remains/Unidentified Human Remains and the True Nature of Love*.

Brad currently divides his time between his homes in Toronto and Edmonton while working throughout the rest of the world.

Brad Fraser plays published by NeWest Press:

Love and Human Remains/
Unidentified Human Remains and the True Nature of Love
Prairie Play Series: Number 15
ISBN 1-896300-04-9
$18.95 pb

Poor Super Man
A Play With Captions
Prairie Play Series: Number 14
ISBN 0-920897-81-9
$13.95 pb

The Ugly Man
Prairie Play Series: Number 13
ISBN 0-920897-43-6
$12.95 pb

The Wolf Plays
contains: *Wolfboy* and *Prom Night of the Living Dead*
Prairie Play Series: Number 12
ISBN 0-920897-49-5
$14.95 pb